Three Kilos of Coffee

Three

An Autobiography

Kilos of

by Manu Dibango

Coffee

In collaboration with Danielle Rouard

Translated by Beth G. Raps

With a Foreword by Danielle Rouard

The University of Chicago Press Chicago and London

Manu Dibango currently lives in Paris with his wife and three children. Among numerous honors and awards, he was made Chevalier des arts et des lettres by the French Ministry of Culture in 1986. **Danielle Rouard** is a journalist for *Le Monde*.

The University of Chicago Press, Chicago 60637
The University of Chicago Press, Ltd., London
© 1994 by The University of Chicago
All rights reserved. Published 1994
Printed in the United States of America
03 02 01 00 99 98 97 96 95 94   5 4 3 2 1

ISBN (cloth): 0-226-14491-7
ISBN (paper): 0-226-14490-9

Originally published as *Trois kilos de café*,
© Lieu Commun, 1989.

Library of Congress Cataloging-in-Publication Data

Dibango, Manu, 1933–
    [Trois kilos de café. English]
    Three kilos of coffee : an autobiography / Manu Dibango ; in collaboration with Danielle Rouard ; translated by Beth G. Raps.
       p.   cm.
    Discography: p.
    ISBN 0-226-14491-7.—ISBN 0-226-14490-9 (pbk.)
    1. Dibango, Manu, 1933–   . 2. Jazz musicians—Biography. I. Rouard, Danielle. II. Raps, Beth G. III. Title. IV. Title: 3 kilos of coffee.
ML419.D53A3   1994
788.7'165'092—dc20
[B]   93-44597
                                           CIP
                                         MN

To those who love me for what I am. To those I love. Without heroes, life is flat. To those heroes who accompany me in my life. They have never been dethroned. They are present throughout the course of these chapters.—M. D.

Contents

Foreword

What schizophrenia!

The French publisher had given me carte blanche; with some ignorance, I chose to write Manu Dibango's biography in the first person. Much later, when the book came out, Manu commented, "When we worked on that book, it was like Danielle raped me." Over months of collaboration, "I" became a reflected image, a hybrid creature. A plump little white journalist relived the life of a great saxophonist and composer in the avant garde of world music, whom she'd never met before. She saw with the eyes of an African, heard with his long ears, laughed and suffered with his heart of a black man.

Our first meeting, with Mr. Dibango and his manager on one couch, and I and my editor on another facing them, resembled a formal introduction between two families. The very next day, Manu and I got together again alone, with no one else around, for the first interview. The test was conclusive for both of us; we decided to commit ourselves to the adventure of this book.

In the humidity of summer, I went to Manu's home regularly for two hours at a time. The hero and his biographer grew tired after that stint, though their concentration was great. Indeed, I insisted on both the silence and absence of the large, noisy tribe that participate in Mr. Dibango's daily existence. I floated the threat of permanently shutting off the tape-recorder to ensure that this single rule was respected.

During sixty hours of interviews, during which Manu recalled aloud the long course of his existence, I only had to stop twice. One afternoon when he was talking about his early life with Coco, who was to become his wife, she sent her little dog Mélodie nosing around the living room where we were working. A few minutes later, Coco entered the room abruptly: "I too have something to say about what we experienced together." I stopped the tape-recorder. Manu apologized to Coco, "It's Danielle . . ." I didn't get upset, but firmly restated the rule I had initially set: "Manu has to finish his story.

And only then, to avoid any falsifications, I'll interview Coco and a few others close to him." Coco left us alone.

A few weeks later, a second incident occurred, which was taken care of just as quickly. Mr. Dibango loves to follow championship tennis, and when he can't get to the stadium, he watches it on television. When I arrived one day, I found Manu glued to the set. Seeing me, he cut the sound but kept one eye on the match. The interview began. His memory failed him—the hero was decidedly elsewhere. I turned off the tape-recorder. "If you talk to me like you're reading the phone book, I'll stop doing this book." The TV went off.

Until the book came out, I shunned anything that could interfere with our working relationship. Mr. Dibango knew nothing more than my telephone number, which was indispensable for setting up our meetings. So, why choose to write this tale in the first person, as a sort of autobiography, short and impressionistic, with Manu as subject, rather than write a heavy biographical tome with Manu as research object?

I didn't make the choice for good until at last, in the solitude of my apartment, I plunged body and soul into my six hundred pages of transcript. Reading and rereading these splashes of memory, hearing and rehearing his voice steering a passage through the never-linear meanderings of a past relived as it was spoken (memory naturally escaping the logic of chronology), I heard music. It was Manu Dibango's music, his "sound" as a man as much as that of his sax. There was no doubt about it. The tale would be told in first-person. The writing, when I started it over, would begin to sound like talking, with no grandiosity. Too bad for the author, who happened to be me; I would disappear, to the greater advantage of this romanesque "I."

Out of concern for clarity, a chronological thread was established. Not a single line reproduced the raw words of the interview, but through the final text an image truer than reality began to filter. When Mr. Dibango read the typed chapters, which I had delivered to him package by package before printing began, he murmured, "that's my sound." When Coco read them in her turn, she was "very moved."

Manu is a man of great modesty, and his memories are more than the repetition of facts. In this book, the saxophonist and composer reviews his past and present life with effort, sometimes, and without complacency. He sketches, as actor and witness, an outline of the history of a continent in full evolution, himself becoming the first of the Africans of Paris, the first of the "Negropolitans" who paved the way for those to come.

Between Europe and Africa, and with frequent incursions into the New World, Manu, as he put it, "vampirized" all music. Over the years he developed the popular, complex music in which the citizens of the world can recognize themselves. For me, this book was above all a journey into his music, using his words.

I decided to retain the use of slang, which Mr. Dibango uses abundantly, with no hint of affectation, preferring to be fanciful rather than dull. He is above all a musician steeped in the jargon of his profession. If sometimes I had to "enrich" this shop-talk where the vocabulary became repetitive, in rereading it, the teller did not feel betrayed.

We went on to compose the chapter titles and section headings. I suggested that Manu use titles of musical pieces, created, as he wrote in his dedication, by "those heroes who accompany me in my life." It was a day of auspicious conception—the titles flowed as from a river.

Then came the time to select photographs for the book, an addition I thought necessary. I had dreamed up a layout and made a preliminary selection of about a hundred unpublished photos from among the five hundred or so that Manu produced from his own collection. Creating the photo section as a family album was important to me and took time. The Dibango family had their say; the publisher imposed constraints as well.

Manu and I worked within a bubble that finally burst. *Three Kilos of Coffee* reached the public, first in France, then in Italy. Here it is in the U.S. While world music floods the continents, this book has gone off on its own journey, independent of its authors. So much the better.

Danielle Rouard

Mr. and Mrs. Michel Manfred N'Djocké Dibango have the honor of announcing the birth of their son, Emmanuel Dibango N'Djocké, in Douala, December 12, 1933, at 11:00 P.M.

Nime̲le̲ Bo̲lo̲

IN THE NEIGHBORHOOD SHACKS and French colonial administration offices of the great port of Cameroon, the refined letters of the parchment sheet announcing a birth are a precious act, worthy of the event itself. On the African continent in the early thirties and coming from a black family, such an announcement was unusual. Emmanuel, son of God, *Imanu* in the Douala translation of the Bible.

Thirty-six years later, this first trace of my history remained with me, hung like an amulet on the wall of my Paris home. The announcement, tinged with pride, gave me to understand early on that I was a wanted child.

My father, a civil servant, was of the Yabassi people. A farmer's son, he had come to my mother's village from far away by pirogue, along the path of rivers. Mama was of the Douala people, born in the city of Douala. This Cameroonian port was the first to know the white man. It was here the first Europeans disembarked. Peasants came from the interior to discover this city and its strange white faces. The Doualas are affected with a certain snobbery and consider the rest of their compatriots savages. Happily, my father found favor in the eyes of his family-in-law; his status as a civil servant certainly helped. But despite his rare and validating social situation, the two families never got along. Both considered the union of different ethnic groups an unsuitable alliance.

My father, married once before to a woman from his region, had a son who stayed with us after his parents separated. Once repudiated, this boy's mother went to live with my paternal uncle, faithful in this to tribal custom. I am my mother's only child. Despite her sorrow and ever-disappointed hopes, she was never able to give her husband further descendants. They accepted this verdict and continued to love each other despite their unhappy fate.

My father and mother were Protestant. They were in love with each other, an exception in a time when a man could marry five or six wives and dispense with love. Their engagement had been a long one. Because he couldn't purchase his wife, my father could have carried her off. But he refused to do so. He preferred to be patient and respect the rules of the period. When the time came, he paid in goats and salt for the right to marry her.

I am a divided man. Born of two antagonistic ethnic groups in Cameroon, where custom is dictated by the father's origin, I have never been able to identify completely with either of my parents. Thus I have felt pushed toward others as I made my own path. It's been easier for me to fill the gap this way, I who was neither foreigner nor completely integrated into my world of origin. I was a broken bridge between two worlds—one part of my being stuck on the eastern shore, the other wandering in the west. In keeping with my astrological sign, Sagittarius, I was passionate about art and had a sense of justice, which I was to abandon in order to return to square one.

My father's elder brother was the head of our extended family. As such, he negotiated the Yabassis' settlement on Douala lands. At his death, my father refused to take over. Just as he had chosen to live only with my mother, he never chose to initiate me fully into the customs of my ethnic group. So I forgot my father's Yabassi language little by little and began to speak only the Douala of my mother, who was raising me. Thus I was divided from the time I was born, part of my history lost in the journey between my father and my mother, the part every man owes it to himself one day to find in a process sometimes called "freedom" or "art."

The Yabassis' encampment was on the Bassa plateau, not far from the Wouri river in the heart of Douala, amid the tumult of steam trains, pirogues plowing the estuary's branches, and English and French bicycles rolling to harbors and markets. Our house was here. Early on its roof was made of palm-fiber mats and later of wood. Sheet metal and concrete succeeded them, following the sequence of African-style "progress." Oil and gas storm lamps were replaced by Petromax gas lamps, which appeared in the same era as the sheet-metal roofs. Here fifteen years of childhood flowed by, spent contemplating the river's course and its possible journeys, following the locomotives to the horizon, their fat white clouds billowing pretty fantasy pictures. I had a fantasy myself: a place I could perhaps draw together and bury my contradictions.

Mamadou and Bineta

When I was a small child, my parents enrolled me in the village school, where I first learned Douala. For this I had just one book with a pink cover, *Nimele Bolo* [*Push the Pirogue*]. In learning to read it, I became familiar with one of my country's main languages. Once classes were over, I would go to church. Like every little Protestant, I discovered the importance of ritual and song. While Luther enlightened my young spirit, my best friends adhered to Catholicism's teachings. They were Boy Scouts and I a Guide. At the least opportunity, quarrels arose between us. And yet, while I couldn't call the Pope a cousin, how I envied my little Catholic friends—they had so much more freedom than I, they who knew nothing of the rather austere charm of Protestant families. At six in the evening, when my father came home from work, he would ring the bell on his bicycle. I stopped playing ball with the others, went home, and didn't come out again. From our compound—that is, our land—I heard my friends dancing, jumping, yelling during nights the moon shone brightly. After sundown, access to the outside world was forbidden to me. What imaginary trips I would take to meet up with my friends; what splendid games we would have until the black night engulfed our bodies! But when the dream was over, I had to think of my classes again and do all I could to succeed in school. My greatest entertainment was music. Even then I had sounds in my head and a particular ability to recall them. I found a kind of gift in myself.

At church, my mother directed the women's choir. I went there myself with my half-brother and a cousin, André Titty, who lived with us. The choirmaster gave me the magical musical virus, while the pastor discussed the Old and New Testaments in their Douala translation. He spoke to us of Jerusalem, of Nazareth; at the time, I thought Paradise must look like Israel. The mystery of Mary and Joseph ("Massa Yo" or "Massa Yosef") fascinated us. A "Massa Yo" in our language was someone who sold bananas and peanuts to people who didn't have time to go home to eat for lack of transportation. (In western Cameroon, the wealthiest people were the ones who started out with three pounds of bananas and ended up with a whole plantation.) I also went to church every evening for religious instruction, or *nkouaïda*, as we called it. Those evenings were like a party, a chance to get out of the house. Yet learning music was not painless: those whose singing was flat got the stick. I remembered voices and harmonies easily. When I went home, nascent conductor that I was, I would make everybody sing. My favorite thing was to marry voices together, creating a human instrument that sounded true and strong. My closest friend had a very low voice. (Years later, I found him again and we pursued our music together.) Once my orchestra conducting was ended, I headed to the gramophone, which I used in secret when my parents were out.

Many people came through our house, all kinds of people who wanted my father's advice. When the law was changed to make the German colony a French protectorate, people needed the changes explained, their forms filled out—all the things necessary to go from an orally based civilization to a written one. Civil servants like my father, who was an official functionary (a title essentially revocable at any time), were charged with smoothing over the numerous administrative hitches. While the role of the section chief was very political—he received the instructions—it was the job of the technicians, who worked directly with the whites, to explain the changes. In such circumstances, someone could have made a lot of money on the sly in "services rendered." A minister's pay wouldn't have met the expenses of many in public life. Some civil servants are like artists—they have to show off, even when their pockets are empty. Mistresses (called "offices") were a minimum.

At our house, my father wrote up the letters every visitor needed. Whole families would come from the bush to ask for his help, bringing enough food for two weeks. If they were sick, my father would help them. He had an open account at the pharmacy, which was no mean privilege. Using his power, he could have cut deals—for example, by buying a taxi and having it driven to make more money—but his moral rigor always forbade his doing so. Still he was very smart, and I was proud of him, with all these people asking for his help.

My mother was a clothing designer. Her husband had bought her some Manufrance sewing machines. She ran her business, hosting many apprentices. What luck for a civil servant to marry a woman who had such taste for design and who already knew how to read and write! I never saw coins or bills exchanged. I simply saw sacks of food enter our house to pay for the apprentices' training. If I wanted a jacket or a pair of shoes, I was made to understand whether there was enough money for it.

My mother was soft, my father hard. He was the one who struck. Very hard. He kept the whip in his room; when I misbehaved, I knew the punishment and went to get the whip. At school, punishment; at church, punishment. My whole childhood was to be marked by this fear of misbehaving. Such a rearing, dispensed by strokes of the stick, marked my sensibilities. Fear of my father never disappeared. Years later, when I received a letter from him, it would take me a week or two to get over his remonstrances. Yet my father loved me very much.

Thus went life on our compound until I got to the whites' school at age seven. Reaching a new level of schooling forced me to learn French. I read the series about Mamadou and Bineta hoeing millet and sorghum. I was very proud to go to the whites' school, which was two kilometers from the compound. I was happy there. The teacher, a man from western Cameroon of an ethnic group in which artists were plentiful, was an extraordinary draftsman and painter.

When the Second World War broke out, we didn't have a radio, but we managed to get some information via the colonialists. My father hid a number of people who fled to avoid being drafted, kicking us children out of bed for them in the middle of the night. It was perfectly awful. But it didn't keep us from singing with my mother and her apprentices all day long. The melodies were not mine, but over time I appropriated them—so much so that when I later heard Bach's *Canticle*, which I'd learned in church, I was sure it was music from home, a song from my country.

"C'est Nous les Gars de la Marine"

With the arrival of the French navy at the port of Douala, Western music erupted on the scene: "C'est Nous les Gars de la Marine" ["It's Us, the Navy Guys"] and Glenn Miller. On the compound, we would put words to the songs in Pidgin; to "In the Mood," we would sing, *"You di wan moni, you di gofo Paris"* ("If you want money, you must go to Paris"). In town, some Africans played traditional music; others worked in the bars and hotels where the whites went. The big port hotel, the Atlantic, had its own musicians, and when they came home at night to the neighborhood, they would teach us all the

popular songs—more or less. Since the white clients were not great
musicians themselves, the Africans playing at their command performed these songs only approximately. In turn, we kids transformed
these approximations from the white district, singing them as we
played ball.

At the time, the Atlantic and Lido hotels were the source of our
musical inspiration. I was never able to go inside, so I had to satisfy
my curiosity with their facades. I caught a glimpse once, when our
group of little Guides marched to celebrate the general's arrival.
(In 1944, de Gaulle came to Cameroon and our school was chosen
to perform at the welcoming ceremonies. We marched by singing,
walking in formation before the hotel, the port, and the fancy European houses.) Just going from one neighborhood to another all
the way to the whites' part of town was a party. Sometimes, forgetting about music, I watched the cycle races. I was crazy about my
maternal aunt's husband, who was a racer. I thought he was so hand-
some and so talented to be able to win so many times. My daily life
was filled with those little adventures that make a childhood and,
over time, retain a pungent perfume. Yet increasing family conflicts
and advice giving were also part of the panorama.

Back then, my mother was sick a lot. I didn't know exactly what
she had. Of course, in the African way, her illnesses were attributed
to the disagreement between the families and the curse on her head.
She often left the house to receive a kind of treatment called *moussala*
in another village. She never gave me her breast; a wet-nurse had
taken me into the fields on her back. This absence of skin contact
with my mother began to seem like a handicap to me, a lack, a little
private wound whose prickings I still feel. In fact, Iyo, my mother's
younger sister, raised me.

"Les Contes de la Brousse et de la Forêt"
(Tales of the Bush and the Forest)
Léopold Senghor

According to tradition, my initiation into my role in society began
with circumcision. When I was about six, my father decided to accomplish it by taking me to the hospital, less barbaric than one of
the *féticheurs*, leaving me there alone because he had to go to work.
In the operating room, amid the nurses, I heard talk of a razor.
Seized with panic, I jumped out of the window and returned to the
compound. At home I faced shame—followed by punishment. Then

I had to go to the village to have it done in the African way: they cut it and bandaged it according to ritual. Only three people were there. All that happened around me before, during, and after was frightening.

My initiation took place at the crossroads between one age and another. The traditions of my two ethnic groups sometimes conflicted; both sides claimed their share in my raising. Many mysterious things cropped up during these ceremonies, and only rarely did I understand their meaning. I was not master of my freedom—I gave in; I was afraid. In fact, I made promises without knowing their consequences for the future. In initiation, you learn abruptly whether you are elect, or chosen, so you know very early on whether "luck" will be by your side in your existence. When you have it, other people don't let you forget it. I began to become aware of it when everything done around me showed I was elect. My new status implied much responsibility; it was very demanding. I became less free in society. As one of the elect, I had to take responsibility for things—a little like my paternal uncle, who had all rights to the house, including over his brother's wife. The clan had to become my major concern. And my responsibility toward my family would only grow over time. In other words, I became the guy who would have to work, to take care of things for the others.

From my initiation onward, I had to live with the burden of being the *mouna moussima*, the "lucky child." This burden would stay with me throughout the thirty years in my trade of "luck" that followed. When I left Douala at fifteen, I didn't know the weight of the promises I had made. I left that country without ever having lived there as a man. I will never be able to say I fulfilled my duties there as my father did before me. I'll never know about the subtle mechanisms that rule ethnic hierarchy. By leaving, I suddenly became a foreigner.

There is a particular promise I didn't keep, so I can speak of it: I was not supposed to return home with a foreign wife. I did. But I paid for it, spiritually and psychologically. When my white wife later came with me to live in Cameroon, getting along with people wasn't easy. We had to be tough to withstand the pressure on us. We were thrown off balance. Even though I was arriving from another country, my behavior still had to be consonant with my society of origin. In circumstances such as these, you have to be very strong and diplomatic, or you risk being devoured by the social machine. France is not the only place where xenophobia exists. In Africa, too, the for-

eigner is suspect. Initiation vows are a code, with laws designed to
protect the community from external dangers. But while they may
bar the path of aggressors, they also hinder the development of one's
own identity.

At my circumcision, the beginning of my initiation, my "luck"
began to show: I was almost never sick. Yet the climate was rough.
When the head is weak, the body may give in. Mosquitoes, ticks, and
malaria all endangered our survival. As kids, we would sometimes
hear adults say, "That guy you were just talking to went home, lay
down, and died." "Oh, yeah, you know, that's what happened to the
guy next door. He ate something bad." Funeral succeeded funeral at
such a pace that you didn't have time to get your clothes cleaned.
Adults would leave work, put on their traditional clothes, and go to
the burial, where they would have a drink. Some took advantage of
the opportunity to transact business there; others looked for dates.
Life continued during the ceremonies of death. Meanwhile I was in
constant fear that my mother would die. "Neighborhood business,"
as we used to say.

Do You Know the Three Colors?

My father said, "I will send the first of my two sons who gets his
certificate to Europe." My half-brother was four years older than I,
but as he started out in the village and went to school well after I
did, we were in the same class. I had to get my diploma before him—
I wanted so much to know the world, to go look beyond Cameroon.
In August 1948 I first learned that my father was dreaming of my
exile. To him, Europe was Paradise. Everything there was done for
the well-being of the whites. There were no earthen buildings, just
cement everywhere, clean. The songs themselves made me dream:
"France is beautiful./Do you know the three colors, the three colors
of France?" My father did not tell me of his plans directly. I caught
snatches of conversation in the house and outside, in the courtyard,
when someone went to get water: "Oh! You're lucky; you're going
to go there." I ended up confirming it for myself with Mama.

As for Papa, he took me to buy my wardrobe, that magical word
that is itself the start of a trip. Three pair of shoes and two suits, one
for summer and one for winter because it would be cold in Europe.
Just to have a suit was to be someone important in Cameroonian
society. In addition, the wardrobe indicated my caste, designated me
as the elect invited to depart for France. By being chosen, I had

become a star in the neighborhood and in school. I hardly slept anymore. I would get up at night to contemplate my suitcases. I missed no opportunity to make my friends drool by telling them about my preparations: "My father took me to the tailor." "How many suits is he having made for you? How many pairs of pajamas?" I who had never worn any! Back home, pajamas symbolized blacks' success in white society. Every Sunday the happy man who owned pajamas would walk to the water wearing them in order to be admired by the community and to give all around to understand that he was "somebody big." There he would majestically groom himself and, once washed, go to Mass. Among all "great men," pajamas were accompanied by a bicycle (preferably English) that made the sound of a clock as its wheels turned. The wife of such a man also possessed a bicycle, even if she did not know how to use it. Superbly dressed, as women always were back home, she could parade around for miles on foot, her machine at her side. Then your buddies would say, "Your mother sure didn't marry a fool, and she sure has money."

My father thus had two pairs of pajamas made for my departure, but he could not afford to purchase those with European labels. Clothing and supplies began to pile up in my bags. The wardrobe list had been established in France by Monsieur Chevallier, a teacher in Saint-Calais in the Sarthe region who corresponded with Titty, my cousin-brother, and who would host me first in France.

I dreamed whole nights through as the departure date approached. I swam in joy and impatience. I thought everyone was rejoicing for me. But no! Of course some people resented me. Jealousy existed. People put curses on me. This mysterious climate frightened me a little, I who mixed my Protestant and animist beliefs. For someone to resent me was like a frightful beast roaming the night. On the advice of a sorcerer, we decided to place offerings outside to ward off fate. Uncle Bébey, my mother's little brother, reassured me. He was so good with his hands; he made little cars for me, I who was so clumsy. Titty helped me too. They were the first ones I would miss.

It rained on my day of departure. The boat I took was the *Hoggar*. Of course I hadn't slept at all the night before. To be fifteen and leaving your country. . . My parents settled me into the cabin and I began to explore the ship, so big and impressive. I had been on whites' steamships before, both to see how they lived and to buy fish. But now Douala was fading away. I was alone, sailing toward the unknown, as I had always wanted. The two families remained on the

quay. They had celebrated my departure for the whole week beforehand. How much we ate, despite the cost of food! Feasts of local
dishes to show off for the neighborhood—*ndolé*, with its slightly
bitter taste, which I adored; *pépé* soup; goat-meat stew; and spicy
n'gondo with dried shrimp or boiled meat. I savored it all, accompanied by *missolès*, fried plantains, and miondos (manioc sticks).

As the siren screamed, my father gave me a small sum and three
kilos of coffee to pay for my first term at boarding school. The
obligatory down payment had already been made. Then the *Hoggar*
pulled away from the Douala estuary toward France, toward Saint-
Calais.

Really the Blues

MEZZ MEZZROW

T HE *HOGGAR* TOOK TWENTY-ONE long days that spring of 1949 to reach Marseilles. I was overcome by seasickness, particularly at the outset. The bitter smells of the ship mixed with those of the sea made my stomach churn, and the food concocted on board gave me nothing but trouble. The food was much different from what I was used to, which caused me to think Cameroonian cooking must be the best in the world. The crossing was lazy. Time took its time. I strained for final images of my country hung on the veil of light sheltering the horizon.

The steamship stopped often. At each layover, I followed the sailors on pub-crawls. I began to discover the world, Africa. In Guinea, I purchased a bunch of bananas to offer as a gift to my hosts. Just before we arrived at Dakar, a Senegalese man got on and sold me a beautiful watch, very costly—seventeen hundred CFA francs. But I was bilked—the watch didn't work.

At last, the *Hoggar* arrived in Marseilles one fine spring day at four in the morning. All the passengers got off and so did I, with my two iron trunks. No one was waiting for me. My host, who was in the military at Montpellier and whom I knew only from his photograph, should have been there. But no. I was utterly confused. Dawn broke. The stevedores unloaded the boat. An old Marseilles local, an "Africa hand," noticed me in tears. Kindly, he took me and my suitcases into an office at the port. The hours went by. I felt lost. Where was my correspondent? Did he mistake the day I was coming? Did he send a letter to Cameroon that we didn't get in time? Finally he arrived at about eleven that morning. He'd missed his train in Montpellier. I had melted into a puddle.

When evening came, we took the train for Paris. Twelve hours we stood—no reserved seats, in a train stuffed to bursting—to the Gare de Lyon. We crossed Paris to get to the Gare Montparnasse for the little train to the Sarthe region. What a disappointment! The buildings were gray. I had heard Paris's charms sung for so long. This was what they called Paradise? It was a real disappointment.

We finally arrived in Saint-Calais at about 9:00 P.M. It was still daylight, whereas in Douala it would already be dark at 6:00 P.M. My hosts, the Chevalliers, tried to send me to bed. I refused. I couldn't go to bed before the moon had risen. I offered them the bunch of bananas I had bought in Guinea in spite of it all. Strange family.

Mr. Chevallier's father, who had gone to the United States during the war, had never come back. There he had become a taxi driver, and he regularly sent both word and money to his wife. Did he have political problems? Romantic ones? No one dared talk about it too much. My correspondent and teacher's grandmother also lived in the house at Saint-Calais. She was very strict, but that was not a big change from what I was used to at home. I stayed at the house ten days, just to get used to things. Then I was enrolled as a boarding student in the technical school at Saint-Calais, where I would attend my second and third years of high school.

I returned to the Chevalliers each weekend. They soon adopted me. I became part of the household, invited to all family gatherings. Such an atmosphere—France at the end of the forties. Comfortably settled in my new home, I enjoyed having my own room. The attic was filled with a packrat's library. I received permission to go there and enjoyed digging deep into adventure stories such as *The Three Musketeers*. Another happy coincidence: the neighbors had children my age.

At boarding school, the first weeks were hard. I underwent a new initiation: hazing. Every new student had to accept "baptism" by the elder ones. At home, the same ritual existed when you entered high school—you didn't have the right to say hello to the elders or even talk to them, or else you were fined. Although I had been warned about similar practices at this school, I was surprised. I had never slept in a dormitory before! I went the whole night without closing my eyes, a slipper under my bed, awaiting the steady step of the one who would surely come to attack me. I kept watch every night for a whole week. Little by little I relaxed and my temper

mellowed. I began to dream of the snow they told me would come
with winter. But it turned out there wasn't any that year. The Chevalliers were disappointed that they couldn't show me France under
snow. I wouldn't see snow until December 1950 in Versailles.

My second and third years went by with good scholastic results.
When I had received my certificate in Douala, I was at almost the
same level as a first-year student here. In Africa, the whites really
pushed us hard, to force the selection process.

At the end of every week, I would go to the Chevalliers and help
out with the chores. I milked cows on the neighboring farm in my
wooden shoes as everyone else did. Returning to boarding school on
Monday, I would take the special foods of my region with me—
Mans-style potted pork, headcheese. My father insisted on paying
my school fees with packages of coffee. In France, amid postwar
penury, people could really use it.

Before I came to Saint-Calais, the locals had never seen a black
person. In town, I thus became an object of kindly curiosity—an
African with the blues. At fifteen, seeing no one of your race made
you long for home. When I got depressed, I imagined returning to
Cameroon; I would be someone there. I lionized my country from
afar. Actually, I missed my parents more than my town.

Concerto for Cootie
Duke Ellington

But what happiness too when I first heard Louis Armstrong hum-
ming on the radio! Here at last was a black voice I recognized, a
voice singing songs like the ones I learned in church.

Radio set the beat of my day-to-day life. Television didn't exist.
We were fervent fans of "Famille Duraton" and Charles Trenet.
When he sang "La Mer" I saw my own country, with women going
to the beach to look for fish. So many memories took me back to my
past; I got tears in my eyes. The few smells that came to me from
my childhood were contained in the letters my father sent me once
a month. My mother didn't write. In his missives, my father gave me
advice: what I should do, whom I should befriend. He forbade me
to correspond with people from home so they wouldn't know where
I was staying; otherwise they might cast spells on me. My father lived
as a Cameroonian; I was already in another world.

But my solitude weighed too heavily on me. I had to meet other
Africans, so I had to learn right away where they were. My corre-

spondents, the Chevalliers, figured it out. With my good report card, I was able to enroll in high school in Chartres at the beginning of the 1950 school year. There I met some Ivoirians and Senegalese who became long-time friends. They had so many hilarious stories to tell. My first African friends always spent their vacations at a resort for Africans. I hastened there in my turn. All the young guests were older than I was. Hardly surprising: in Africa, to get into the whites' schools, you have to lie about your age. These Ivoirians were used to subterfuge. They were already shaving, and some had even known women. On Saturdays, their sole concern was to lay their pants flat under the bed to press them and then to dress up elegantly to go dancing. We kids of seventeen watched them primping in secret. We made fun of them, all the while fearing the blows they might give us.

My series of journeys to the various French holiday resorts for young people began in this period and lasted until 1956. I discovered an idyllic France where racial tension was absent. My African friends were there to go to school, not to work, and everyone knew it. To me, these Africans were "lucky." They were the sons of wealthy families. Some paid nothing; their parents, members of the upper class, were able to get them scholarships. My father, merely middle class, was not able to do so. Such scholarships were worth twice as much as those given to the French students. And the Indochinese students were as rich as Croesus. They had more money than they knew what to do with. In this period, France had enormous trafficking in currency. The earliest students from the countries of the French Empire (the *Union Française*) to possess Vespas and cameras were the Indochinese. Their good fortune made the little French kids from the provinces scream. Without quite as much money as they, we Africans lived in ease. Everything was paid for, even our vacations. Our parents also sent us pocket money, further gilding our youth. It took real willpower not to slip into the surrounding ease, and to resist the temptations of the sweet life of a student free from familial authority.

I felt much more at ease among my own. I could finally breathe the perfume of connection bonding me to my new friends in exile. I had just turned seventeen. I was already picking out notes on the mandolin and beginning to learn piano. I took lessons from a teacher at the high school in Chartres. My father wanted to refine my education without making a musician of me; he would never wish such a miserable goal on his son.

Christmas 1950 came, and off I went to a holiday camp at Versailles. I smoked my first Craven and Elégant cigarettes. Easter holidays at Saint-Germain-en-Laye. I started going to dances. The following summer I went back to Saint-Germain-en-Laye. Cameroon, proud of its special status, had opened a camp so its children didn't have to mix with other Africans. Here I met Francis Bébey. I already had a love for music; he shared his passion for it with me and introduced me to jazz. A few years my elder, Francis fell in love with one of my cousins, whom he ended up marrying. Later, returning to his origins, he moved away from jazz.

Among the Cameroonians during this summer vacation of 1951 were many who loved music. Some loved to dance; others loved to play. Some preferred the mambo beat—Latin music, which was very popular then. Francis and I tended toward jazz. Together we mounted our first amateur group—or at least we started to. Francis played guitar very well; I kept up on mandolin and piano. We put together a band the way other kids would a soccer team. Without being overly serious about it, we did pretty well on our instruments. Francis taught me the first scale the blues are based on. He explained the twelve measures to me, taught me harmony, and finally revealed the universe of Duke Ellington to me. Enchanted, I bought my first record, *Concerto for Cootie*. Francis started to exert the magic my choirmaster in Douala had held for me when I was a child. Francis and I loved each other. I admired him, and he displayed to me the interest of a teacher for his student. Also in Saint-Germain-en-Laye that summer, I hung out with Jean-Gaston Noah, Yannick's uncle, and with N'Joh Léa, who was getting into soccer as we were moving toward music.

Alas! Our happy holiday ended. Each of us had to go back to boarding school. Whenever we could, we got back together to play at student dances in Provins, Montargis, and Reims. I had other friends at school, but I didn't feel the same joy in their company. My music professor took a shine to me and allowed me to play piano after lunch. At the end of the first semester, three of my friends hopped the wall and got kicked out. In solidarity, I too left the school, which sent us hunting for another port of refuge. Rambouillet opened its doors, but there again one of us was not accepted because of bad test scores. We went to Paris for a few days and wound up admitted to La Fontaine High School in Chateau-Thierry.

One January night at 4:00 A.M. I set my bags down in Chateau-Thierry. The station was haunted by a wind engulfing us through broken panes. I settled in for two years at La Fontaine. I devoted more time to music but also started having girlfriends. In the summer of 1952, all of expatriate Africa gathered in Saint-Hilaire-du-Harcouët, a camp near Granville. Zogbo, an Ivoirian, directed the show that we planned to present at the Granville casino. I was in charge of piano accompaniment. Finally the great night arrived. Mick Micheyl was singing on stage—we were in ecstasy.

I also discovered the saxophone at Saint Hilaire, thanks to Francis Kingué, a compatriot and student at Bagnères-de-Bigorre who played solo in the casino's large band. Francis had a colorful accent and a beautiful golden alto sax. As his fans, we felt the purest admiration for him. At the same time, we were crazy about American jazz players. Miles Davis worked the trumpet differently from Armstrong. Johnny Hodges made his alto sing with Duke's band differently than Charlie Parker did. This was the beginning of the quarrel between the old and new schools that would fracture jazz history. We all wanted to play alto—some like Hodges, others like Parker. One of my friends loaned me a silvery sax (perhaps to keep me from playing piano!). From 7:30 A.M. on, I would play like a madman and break everyone's eardrums. I never let go of that sax and never paid for it. In later years, when I saw him in Yaoundé, its owner would regularly remind me, "Hey man, you owe me!"

At first, I didn't really like the instrument all that much. It tickled my lips. But aside from nice long walks, how better to pass the time? On my return to La Fontaine, I enrolled in a sax class.

Jammin' the Blues

I left Chateau-Thierry for Reims in 1953 and continued my private lessons with another professor. There I had an astounding meeting with Van Put, a very gifted accordionist—phenomenal. When he played his thing he put so much into it that he made me love the tango almost in spite of myself. The guy deserved a halo as far as I was concerned. His music spoke. Every Saturday night and Sunday he would bring the music to life at the club in town where he played. I followed his every step. One thing led to another, and he had me play a number on my sax. The owner responded by paying me a little. I became a hit in Reims! I was the only African who played sax, albeit clumsily.

My list of idols grew longer. I became an imitator—hat and suit like Lester Young, holding my cigarette and blowing smoke rings like him. Though Tino Rossi was all you heard on the airwaves, American blacks captivated me. They were my heroes—those black boxers, for example. When Sugar Ray Robinson had his night fight at New York City's Polo Grounds, we switched on the radio, even though it was 4:00 A.M. our time. One of us had a radio and made the others pay to hear the broadcast of the fight. Sugar Ray was coming to fight in Paris? We stood in line to catch a glimpse of him. He was a real star. The newspapers burned up with tales of his personal hairdresser and his strawberry, raspberry, and candy-cane Caddies. He posed with Martine Carol and other stars. Our idol had his hair conked. Immediately, we too "burned" our hair; some lost it all.

In France, everyone was mad for Chester Himes, the black novelist from New York. In our adolescent eyes, he was the fantasy of the black man who had made it, who was at the same level as the rest of the Western world, since we African kids didn't have heroes from our own continent. The hour of independence had not yet struck. Armstrong, Sidney Bechet, the Lesters were like gods to us—more to us than to their fans in Saint-Germain-des-Près, where they would give concerts.

To get closer to our music, we deserted our holiday camps for Paris. I went in with a friend on what had once been a maid's tiny one-room apartment at number 11, Place de la Nation. Our whole group was inebriated by these Parisian nights. This was the era when Saint-Germain was at its peak. We wandered around until dawn, going from the Black and White—the first black club in the capital—to the Louisiane Hotel—with its colonial charm, where the members of international jet set would come to stay—to the Montana—where everyone who was anyone in Paris had to show up at cocktail hour. Paris movie houses were showing *Jammin' the Blues*, in which the world finally saw the jazz kings' faces. On stage in the cabarets, the Frères Jacques blew everyone away. Claude Luther played at the Lorientais. Juliette Gréco was a heartthrob, singing lying down in a coffin in the dark at the back of a Portuguese club on Rue de Verneuil. Modern jazz at the Chat Qui Pêche and the Caméléon; traditional at the Huchette and the Vieux Colombier; blues at the Trois Maillets; bebop everywhere. And since this beat ran in their own blood, Cameroonians were champs at getting the chicks.

We made the rounds of the clubs without a dime to our names. We tried to slip into the Trois Maillets. Its doorman, an old Chinese guy, saw nothing strange—we would pass each other the only ticket in our possession, and since we were all black. . . To eat, we used the same stratagem with the Chinese man guarding the entrance to the university cafeteria. Sometimes we had a place to stay at Place Denfert-Rochereau with Lydia Ewande, one of the first African actresses to work in Paris, on stage at the time with Martine Carol. My head was nearly bursting from all this music. But I valiantly continued to prepare for my exams!

"Le Chanteur de Mexico"
Luis Mariano

The word *independence* began to titillate our African minds. Famous folk came from faraway continents to visit us at our holiday camps. The wind of independence was blowing, magical. We felt the breeze in 1954, when some French friends died in Algeria. I started to become aware of the real world. My thoughts awakened to human problems.

Right from the start in this exiles' milieu, other Africans had been somewhat envious of Cameroonians. They had always had a thing about us—maybe because of the special treatment the French-speaking world had given my country? This slight difference disappeared in the fun of the dances we organized. Our elders managed to bring out the stars of popular song: the diaphanous Marie-Laurence, singing a bolero tune in 1953; the Caribbean biguine, which took us by storm; Luis Mariano's hit, "Le Chanteur de Mexico" ["The Singer from Mexico"]; Perez Prado, the mambo king. All this music ran together and made France a magical place. Everyone black pressed into the Petit Balcon, the Bikini, and the *bals nègres*. So many parties!

Like everyone else I danced. But I wasn't great at it—I preferred listening to the music. The dances took place in stages: bolero, waltz, tango, paso doble, and then a series of slow songs, closing with a swing—my favorite. As soon as a musician would start to play one of these, I would stop dancing and looking for women so I could listen better.

"Blues in Third"
Sidney Bechet and Earl Hines

The first year of my two major high school exit exams, I moved to Reims. The city was crawling with American military guys who had been quartered at the surrounding bases since the Liberation—a dream clientele for the clubs. I managed to get myself hired at the Monaco, one of the "in" Reims night spots. On Saturday nights, I would set up jam sessions for the foreign clients; the owner was happy with me. The band leader called me "Sax" in a friendly way. My friends took advantage of my time on stage to approach women. "He's my brother"—what a great line! When my song was over, I would be alone, without having done any "business" myself. At closing, the owner would pay me a little. He offered me a new contract right away. He arranged jazz and popular-music concerts every Sunday from eleven to noon at the Alhambra de Paris. We were off: on Sundays at 7:00 A.M. we would leave the Monaco for Paris. The truck had a strange internal heating system—a pipe open directly onto the motor. What a stench! We would play the Alhambra and return to Reims that night. Thus my reputation was born: "There's a black guy playing there". . . My offers increased; sometimes I would play at the Cerisaie, a bandstand. When I returned to school on Monday morning, I was hardly fresh. My relations with my teachers became a bit strained, but to my friends I was a hero. They would ask me to play at parties in the wine cellars of Champagne, the area where Reims is. I played all the grape harvests; it was really fun.

Despite my initial success, I was still not planning to become a professional musician. I wanted to do well in school so I could go back to Cameroon. But quite naturally my emphasis had shifted from school to music. I began to go to the Jockey Club, where American musicians would play from time to time. To me, all Americans were jazzmen. When one of them broke the rule, I was very disappointed. The army itself gave concerts. Reims was jubilant. She was my source, my window and passport to the world. After passing my first exam, I took a room in town on Rue Chanzy. Of course I failed my next exam, in philosophy. I was living at the center of a whirlwind sucking me in, certain that my fall would come hard. But as my parents were far away, the man in me began to affirm himself. My father's recriminations, though they disturbed me, didn't keep me awake at night. Failing the exam shocked me, though.

On my return the next year, I reenrolled in the course to pass the second-year exams and also enrolled at the Ecole Supérieure de Commerce. What a work load! The idea of becoming a professional musician never even occurred to me. I persisted in my thinking and signed on the line.

Catastrophe came: my father brutally cut off my stipend. Winter

1956 was looming. My parents had heard about my failure in philosophy. A French musician from Reims traveling in Cameroon visited them. He rubbed salt in their wounds: "Your son is a good musician." What could have been a compliment came as an affront. My father had lost face, he who had always seen me coming home to take a high position. But to have sacrificed himself for a son who would become a musician—no. My father sent me a terrible letter in which he told me of his decision: "You are dishonor itself. I can't do this anymore." Henceforth, no more boarding school. As for myself, I was merely afraid of being damned.

"Morning Glory"
DUKE ELLINGTON

I finished the school year as best I could on Rue Chanzy. My Ivoirian friends from Chartres were also living in Reims. We were inseparable. We were interested in politics, and we caught all of Jean Grandmougin's afternoon radio editorials. He had such a great voice. All the Africans would listen to him, not realizing that he was an extremist. When African politicians came through Paris for meetings, we drank in their words. We were there whenever black Africa gathered.

Polemics inflamed jazz. The French imposed jazz on the Americans themselves. Hugues Panassié expended a ridiculous amount of money and a lot of love on his magazine, the *Bulletin du Hot Club de France*. For him, jazz meant the cotton fields. He fought with Charles Delaunay, who defended a more modern jazz in his magazine *Jazz Hot*. Complete amateurs, we devoured all this French writing, so as to miss none of the quarrels of our time. Then Daniel Filipacchi started up a third magazine, *Jazz Magazine*, and the first specialized radio show on Europe 1. At last, a show without a lot of talk that just played the music!

A wealth of information—whichever musician was under discussion, there was something to say. Thus an antiwhite racism was born within jazz and in Paris. To Hugues Panassié, only blacks could make jazz, and only blacks suffered. That didn't make sense to me. In my opinion, Stan Getz, who was white, played admirable sax. I didn't like this kind of taking sides, and I have always been hesitant to hang out among those to whom arguing is like breathing. What a scandal when Parker came on the scene—the battle raged between those "pro" and those "anti." Miles Davis himself did not escape our imprecations. Aimé Barelli said of him, "He plays off-key; he doesn't know how to play trumpet."

I disliked people who intellectualized jazz to the point that it became antiseptic. They didn't make the music, and they were content to drone on through the inventions of the American musicians. One might as well have taken a plane to go hear the Americans themselves in New York City, where zillions of saxophonists could be found in the phone book.

Of course at this time I had neither the means, nor the desire, nor even the dream of doing so. I was happy to buy records and run around to concerts. Count Basie, Duke, Coltrane, Parker—some of their songs marked me for life. I ended up discovering the world through music. In the years to come, these musicians would remain with me; I would never meet better than they. I remained faithful. My heroes will never be dethroned.

I shared this passion with my Ivoirian friends Patrice Nouama and Aimé Barou. In these hard times at the close of 1956 and the start of 1957 in Reims, we feared the worst. But I remained "lucky." Barou had a cousin named Fax Clark, a trumpet player who owned a famous nightclub in Brussels, the Tabou. With students from many countries, Fax had been a part of the first African dance performance to be seen in Paris. Under the direction of Keïta Fodeba, the troupe was now on tour in Italy and northern Europe. One night, Barou incited me to leave France. "In Brussels, you could enroll at the university. Fax is looking for African musicians for his club." The Belgian bourgeoisie and nobility were crazy about the Tabou. They enjoyed African performers. Their only colony, the Belgian Congo, was starting to rumble after a few jolts. Being French and happily not Congolese, I easily obtained a permit to get into the country.

It gave me hope. I left France for Belgium at the end of October, having passed my exams. I held fast to the idea of pursuing my studies while earning a living. Deprived of options, I had no other solution.

"Indépendance Cha-Cha"

BRUSSELS GLEAMED WITH CLEANLINESS, "For
Rent" signs everywhere. What a change from Paris . . .
Right in the first week, I moved into a comfortable apartment
on Rue de Pépin in the Porte de Namur area, twinkling with a thousand lights. Soon after I went to work for Fax. He paid me gener-
ously—two hundred francs a day, twice the fee in Paris. His Tabou
was the kind of club where I had to play all types of music, which
bugged me. But the band was good, and we had a great time on the
jazz numbers. A traditionalist, Fax preferred Armstrong; we preferred Parker. We got on like cats and dogs. I played the standards
on my alto sax and survived musically only by listening to my idols'
records. But at least I was being paid regularly.

The band would start playing at ten and stop when the last customers left to go to sleep. In one short week, I abandoned my plans
to enroll at the university—without regrets. Good-bye to diplomas
and careers! Barou, the one who introduced me to his cousin Fax,
accomplished another *coup* by marrying a woman from Reims. The
world was smiling on me. I lived at a fast pace, between the luxurious
Tabou and my apartment, a stone's throw away. My life as a man
began; I dove into nightlife. I met lots of people because of all the
concerts I went to. As a music lover and lover of musicians, I had
people cover for me at the Tabou when I had the chance so I could
go hear others jam in the bars in the lower part of the city. Belgium
hummed in its bones from all the jazz activity; France seemed slug-
gish by comparison. As soon as the last note fell at a concert I would

approach my distant heroes, but I didn't dare speak to them. I was incredibly shy. It would be a long time before I convinced myself that I could hold my own though others may play well. When my turn on stage came, I would panic and sweat bullets.

Nor did my days know any respite: two subtitled American movies in the afternoon; scales on my sax; trips to record shops, where I made the rare jazz finds Brussels seemed full of, much more so than Paris.

A scant two months after beginning at the Tabou, I was again in "luck." I met the one who never more would leave my side, the one whom I would marry—Marie-Josée, whom I decided to call "Coco."

"Cool Blues"
CHARLIE PARKER

Coco was really beautiful. A model and actress, she was then separated from her husband, a Frenchman and well-known photographer. She also took photos, doing a series of portraits of me. After I put away my sax, we got acquainted. She started coming to my apartment a lot. We decided on 7 February 1957 to stay together. Coco became my eternal guardian angel. She believed in me more than I dared to believe in myself. She did everything for me, always seeking the best for me. While I was playing at the Tabou, she would be running around to concerts to find my American idols. They would try to pick her up, but she was just trying to get them to the club to jam with me. That's how I was able to play with Count Basie's trumpet players. Coco and I had a very stable life together.

But with Fax, things were heating up. In three months, our breakup was complete. He was mad for Broadway and I for Harlem; our fantasies clashed. The struggle between older and younger generations was played out by Africans living in Europe. The bandleader refused to play bebop; he was strictly an Armstrong man. I had no clarinet, just my alto sax. New Orleans style was OK for one piece, but then I would really start to get mad. After just three months at the Tabou, I was through.

Two months of unemployment went by—the only gap in my whole career as a musician in Europe. Kat Kuadjo, who worked with Fax Clark, also had had a fight with the Tabou's owner for the same reasons I had, and then he tried to open a club. I followed him. It was a fiasco. But there I met Emile Letellier, a multi-instrumental bandleader with contracts to play at American bases in France, Germany, and the rest of Europe.

Festival Jesters

Emile Letellier played guitar like Django Reinhardt—marvelously—as well as trumpet and piano. He was incredibly gifted, slightly anarchic. The drummer sat in on trombone with me on sax, a little vibraphone, and piano. The three of us played pieces arranged for six. This was very useful, because it meant that I learned my stuff from the well-known standards. On the American bases, to which we traveled nonstop, I could finally play the music I loved. We would play two hours a night, then sleep at the base. On our rare days off we went back to Brussels. There we spent some wonderful hours with our ears glued to the radio for jazz broadcasts such as "Miles Davis Live." Our travels to the bases ended after three months.

Joe Brown, of Congolese and European descent, then made me a new offer: two months at the Moulin Rouge in Ostend. Joe had lived in Belgium since his childhood and had been a very popular boxer earlier in his life. Black musicians—Africans, preferably—were now all the rage. Joe put me in charge of getting a band together. And there we were at the Moulin Rouge, not for three months but for five. We accompanied all the dancers' acts, which changed every two weeks. So much music to stuff into your head! The club owner was indefatigable—and a total money addict.

One night at 3:00 A.M. we were getting ready to pack it in. He looked outside with his field glasses, and as soon as he spied a boatload of tourists in the distance he yelled, "Let's have some music! The freight's on its way!" We picked up our instruments and played until seven.

I left the Moulin Rouge in September 1957 for the Scotch, a club in Antwerp. There I met Roberto Cortez, a strange Peruvian who pretended he was Cuban and sang in Spanish the Latin American tunes that people were so crazy about—the cha-cha, salsa's ancestor. I joined Roberto's little band. He jealously guarded the secret to a special kind of arrangement. Once the piece had been played, he would take back the sheet music—and there was no reading of the other musicians' parts, either. During breaks at the Scotch, I would hide in the bathroom copying his arrangements to learn how to make a band sound right.

Exit Roberto. I continued my meanderings through the lands of the *Gilles de Binche*, those Belgian festival figures. I snagged a contract for two years at the Chat Noir, a club in Charleroi. It seemed its owner had indeed once heard of a black man who played sax. . . From 1958 to 1960, I played at the Chat Noir, where my existence was that of an O.S. [a semiskilled worker] in music. Among other things, this job ensured that my long-term stay papers would be renewed periodically. Brussels remained my home base. Every evening I would take the train to Charleroi. I arrived there at five to ten and went on five minutes later. During my fifteen-minute break, I would eat a plateful of something among the B-girls working the club. That wasn't quite my style, but in this trade, I couldn't be too picky. There were three of us on stage. The organist was at the pedals and also sang. Since we had no time to rehearse during the day, we would just play to make the customers dance and try to figure out our sheet music. We had no choice. At five before 5:00 A.M. I would get out of there to catch the first train—five brief minutes to put my instrument away, get to the station, and jump into the compartment. When I arrived in Brussels at six, I gave myself time for drinks with my friends in the musicians' bars. I didn't get home until around nine. Sundays were a real achievement: from three to five I added in a tea dance, and at nine I was off to the club again.

Two hard years went by like this with no day off, driving back and forth over snowy roads when the trains were on strike—good years. I got my first car, a gigantic lemon-yellow American number. Sometimes I would escape for a visit to Paris with my student buddies. My good life amazed them; I must have had a "lucky star." Yet I was unable to ask myself what I was going to do in the future, just as I didn't know whether or not I should continue to be a musician. A wave was carrying me along, and the shores of Cameroon were still far away. My parents wrote to me about the country. Peace had come once again, and my mother only had one child. . . Sometimes I would dream of leaving everything to go back to them. More reasonably, I tried to set money aside so I could take a vacation to Cameroon one day.

Then strong shock waves began to shake the political world. The war in the Congo had just broken out. Belgian ex-colonialists returned to Brussels carrying with them the first racial tensions that would later consume Europe. Far too absorbed in my work, I kept apart from the African politics that soon submerged Africa and part of Europe.

I was swimming in my own dreams, my reality bobbing to the beat. At the moment, I identified with Milt Jackson, the Modern Jazz Quartet's vibraphonist. I copied his style and planned to buy myself a vibraphone of the same make. What a funny love affair! I saved up like an ant, all the while singing like a grasshopper. Every week I went to the shop to look at the instrument I wanted to buy for myself. I think I actually adored that vibraphone more than the sax. Later I played it a lot. It gave me immense satisfaction. When synthesizers really became important to music, I felt a less sensual curiosity for them than I do now—the curiosity of someone who loves sound, but not that of a music lover. Such impatience I felt to get my vibraphone . . . but it did go away. I kept my desire to set hands on the piano again. But this love was always conflictual, since I was not a great pianist. Could I still continue to dream of *some* instrument? Over the years, the band became my instrument, a vehicle to realize a vision I could share with others.

Tropicals Among the Typical

In the year 1960 all the political luminaries of Brussels, the European capital, were shining brightly. The Round Table was held here; under the aegis of the UN, discussions about the independence accords between Brussels and the Congo took place. The governors of newborn Zaire ran to Brussels. In town, little islands of African culture popped up. The Anges Noirs was the hot spot where the politicos hung out. Of course, Zairean musicians began stopping by. For the first time, an African band left Zaire to record in Europe: African Jazz arrived with its full complement under the watchful eye of its famous leader, Zairean singer Joseph Kabasele, who spent his evenings at the Anges Noirs.

This was the blessed moment when Fonseca, owner of that club, offered me the chance to lead his house band. What a gift; I'd always wanted to arrange. I was nearly his employee—Fonseca even gave me a month's vacation! Life was easy without being opulent. I began arranging for the band. The Anges Noirs was *the* place to be seen in Brussels, like Régine's in Paris. You had to be sponsored to be a member. The place was frequented by an exceedingly hip crowd—black and white, Belgians and African politicians, with a few rare and lucky students thrown in.

The Anges Noirs's sound was like no other. Brilliantly sunny music, great to dance to, it went way beyond the nearby Enfants

Terribles club, which played the usual stuff. That club was the other chic spot in the upper part of the city. The Anges Noirs's specialty was inviting all the black stars coming through Brussels to sit in. They gave the place its strange new sound. Cubans, Peruvians, Jamaicans, and black Americans encountered Africans. All brought their own repertoires and sang. Our band backed up this whole musical world. Every current in black music was present—an incredible draw, an absolute ferment of creativity! We created a very hot kind of pseudo-African music in Belgium, in total ignorance of the kind of music actually being made in Africa. Throughout this whole period, I kept flying from tea dances to galas. I was even able to take part in Gilbert Bécaud's Belgian tour.

Each evening, I returned to the Anges Noirs for our permanent party. In Zairean tradition, wealthy music lovers had to prove their devotion by sending cases of beer up to the stage. This was how I got close to famous figures such as Patrice Lumumba, Tshombé, Bomboko, and Kalonji and their retinues. It seemed as though a whole world was about to collapse, while war continued on the [African] continent.

The Colonialists Come Home

On their return, the Belgians talked about the war's horrors, its rapes. It was an eye-opener. Until this revelation, I had heard those around me talk about independence, but never had I understood the sorrows and sacrifices it implied. Now I learned the price history would exact. Every day we learned of new conflicts tearing apart the different ethnic groups in their attempts to gain power in the birth of a nation. It was true that whites released power politically without releasing it economically; it was also true that Africans took a while to catch on to the process. They went from words to action, paying with blood.

I wound up experiencing this destruction in my own neighborhood. First my tires were slashed. Then my relationship became the target of a few crazies: Coco and I were one of the few mixed couples in the area. The colonialists had a hard time tolerating us, accustomed as they were to their entrenched apartheid in Léopoldville, which had been renamed Kinshasa upon independence. I was already paying for having betrayed my initiation promises. Our neighbors protected us; they gave the police reports praising us.

The tension created a diffuse kind of fear around the world of the night. We became hesitant to go out at night. The Anges Noirs lost part of its local clientele but gained another: the masses of diplomats, who were better protected. In the fever gripping Brussels, I discovered "Congo" music. The Anges Noirs was the only place in town where Zairean musicians could really get down. The club had always welcomed all kinds of music. In fact, its owner had recently brought over the real biguine from the Canne à Sucre, a white club in Paris. His wife, a singer, was from Martinique. Our band expanded its stock of Caribbean tunes. Sometimes we played with a bassist or a drummer from Guadeloupe. Actually, no music was really dominant in our band. I remained one of the rare members to prefer jazz; more elaborate and more subtle, it was my own kind of classical music.

One night, Joseph Kabasele and African Jazz arrived on the scene at the cavernous Anges Noirs, illuminating it like sunlight. All of Brussels, all of Africa, was kicking up its heels at the time to "Indépendance Cha-Cha," African Jazz's hit about Zaire's brand-new independence. In this piece, the musicians listed the names of all those who had participated in the Round Table discussions. No need to look in the papers—all you needed was the record to know it all. (In Africa, musicians have traditionally played the role of journalists. They chronicle daily events, their music broadcasts the news, and everyone enjoys it. First you hear the music with your feet; then it gets up to your head.) The same thing would happen again through song much later in the fight against AIDS.

"Indépendance Cha-Cha" took its inspiration from two beats— the cha-cha and the rumba, the two breasts nourishing Zairean music. This music—guitars and a duo of singers—had its own harmonic infrastructure. The rumba from the Congo Basin had its own harmonies, rhythm, and melody. Strongly influenced by Latin American music, its words were sung in Lingala, a language that works well to music. The Congolese rumba was a favorite in Brussels; Congo music was the only kind that traveled so easily throughout Africa and Europe. Hardly a surprise—the Belgians, who thought they were going to be living in Léopoldville for a long time, built a huge radio transmitter tower there that broadcast across thousands of kilometers until four in the morning. Since nighttime was when people really lived in Africa, everyone tuned in to Radio Léopoldville. This was how the first African stars became well known—all Congolese-Zairean, of course. Thus were born Kabasele and his band, African Jazz—a strange name, since the band didn't play any jazz at all. But in Africa, *everything* was jazz (in the original meaning of the word), from jazz doctors to jazz hairdressers.

Meeting Kabasele was the first in a lucky sequence of events. The Zairean leader liked my sax playing and invited me to take up Congo music. To tell the truth, I knew almost nothing of its charms. I had only a vague memory of it from Courchevel in 1955, when a buddy had made me listen to a rumba record made in the Congo on which a superb sax solo stood out. At the time I had been surprised that there were musicians in Africa who could play the instrument so well. Only later did I learn that the sax player was Fud Candrix, a one hundred percent lily-white Belgian.

Now aged twenty-seven in 1960, I found the challenge lacking neither novelty nor danger. I had never played a single piece written by my African neighbors. While I understood the music, I couldn't really say I was familiar with it. Yet jazz, an exceptionally useful tool for understanding other musical universes, allowed me to decipher without much difficulty the true nature of the music I was being offered. In fact, Kabasele was the one who opened up Africa to me. Thus, in a strange kind of give-and-take, I returned home not via Cameroon but on the path the Zairean bandleader had cleared for me.

On the continent, the wars of independence continued to blaze. In spite of their violence, the rest of us expatriates felt we were being born anew. We felt a certain pride in our freedom that called us to return home en masse. All of us went with our own little dreams reawakened. For my part, I started thinking of returning to Cameroon to open not a nightclub but a musical conservatory.

While we were dreaming of our future, many of our friends were starting to pursue degrees or political careers faster than fast. Never a clever politician or a subtle diplomat at managing my career, I myself was content to make music. I had no vocation as a fairy-tale frog-prince; I returned quickly to reality. I was a simple African musician set down in an exceptional historical configuration. My connections with Kabasele became closer and closer. From this decisive relationship only a revolution could come. I felt it coming—I hoped.

But history held one of its secret surprises for me.

Côte d'Ivoire, Pride of Africa

The call of the continent came to me indirectly. One hot evening in June 1960, my Ivoirian best friend from France called on me at the

Anges Noirs. Yves Beugré was a guitarist by profession. He and his percussionist brother had a student band in Paris. The Côte d'Ivoire was getting ready for its first independence celebration on 4 August. Yves was to perform at it with his band, and he suggested that I come with them. The Anges Noirs would be closed in August for vacation, so I decided to attend the birth of the Ivoirian nation. Strangely enough, I discovered love of country not in Cameroon but in Abidjan. My past helped me. In France I had lived mostly among Ivoirians and been considered an adoptive Ivoirian. Among them I had met a funny guy, a white man who was close to Houphouët-Boigny. He would make frequent trips to Abidjan and bring back news for this one and that: "I saw your father the other day . . ." As a child, I had dreamed of someone who could say things like that to me. He traveled miles over the French highways to keep in touch with us. Houphouët-Boigny held a national memorial service for this man when he died. He made me love Africa, and especially a country that wasn't even mine—Côte d'Ivoire.

En route to 4 August. Yves organized the trip with the help of some established Ivoirian musicians in Paris. I trembled with impatience thinking about the task awaiting me—playing the first celebration of independence. Coco was part of a dance company planning a tour in Lebanon. Our impending separation carried with it a serious risk: Would our love withstand our separation?

The band took off from Brussels to Abidjan via Paris and Dakar. Abidjan, Dakar—it was all the same to me. In my eyes, Africa was one and not yet many. By mishap the plane was stuck on the ground in Dakar for forty-eight hours. Air France put us up in a hotel (Air Afrique didn't exist yet), and we took the opportunity to wander around. My last visit to the Senegalese capital—in 1949, when the *Hoggar* docked there for a few hours—had left me without memories. In my meanderings I made a stop at the post office and came upon a French woman I knew from high school in Chateau-Thierry who had moved to Senegal. She hardly deigned to speak to me! I couldn't understand why she was so unpleasant. But Africa had already changed her. Firmly set in her colonial ways, she had chosen sides. I had to come to Dakar to feel, personally and for the first time, the rejection I had only vaguely sensed before. In France, I had lived in a cocoon. Of course, like so many others, I had read *Really the Blues*, in which Mezz Mezzrow described the very difficult life of American jazzmen. But after all, those were American blacks. It was a rude awakening in Dakar. Then the plane was repaired and we took off again for Abidjan. There I stayed with Yves's family; his uncle ran the train station.

Abidjan in 1960 was like a small town. I was very well received, but our music—the reason for the trip—took a few knocks. Apparently the Ivoirians who were to take charge of us didn't want to do so, and they had other responsibilities. We were lost; misadventure dogged us. We couldn't even play, for our equipment hadn't arrived. Fights broke out with the local musicians. They thought, "Who do they take themselves for, this bunch of students from Paris?" On Independence Day we did manage to play in spite of everything, but one local band cut off our electricity and another one cut our amp cords. (The number of people in my life who have cut the cords around me is crazy.) After this, troubles came thick and fast. My astral phase must have been negative; the forces of evil had the upper hand. We were in a tight corner, but the stakes were still high. I was happy to be in Africa, happy to meet the first African president and his ministers, all those people I had heard about in Brussels.

My plane ticket allowed stopovers, and it was now or never to see my parents after twelve years away. I flew to Cameroon, landing one dark night at six o'clock. My parents met me at the tiny airport of Douala. They were happy; their son was back. But I sensed a certain nervousness in them that surprised me. Then my father told me we had to get home as fast as we could because Cameroon was under curfew starting at 6:30. I spent a few days in the neighborhood, then left for Brussels, full of sadness. My parents had reminded me of my vow and my social responsibility toward my family. I belonged to a particular order in the world—a world in which people were careful to keep its outlines well defined.

Staying in Brussels, I picked up my work again. The horizon brightened a little. Coco was still in Lebanon, but her letters reached me easily. Finally she came home. We thought carefully and put our counters back to zero.

After making this hard trip to Africa, I was even more interested in Cameroon. I began to dream of returning to Africa. With my savings, I sent presents to my parents. This was my way of proving to them that I was independent. I ended up loving my family very deeply, beyond what was reasonable. I became a pushover. In Africa, "nice" means "weak." Society is unceasingly confronted with its own need to survive. Be nice to your houseboys and your cooks and they'll steal from you because you're weak. We musicians, who give and create out of love, are considered the weakest. Artists must be able to succeed materially in Africa; only then are we respected by others for becoming as tough as our compatriots. Franco, the Zairean musician, inspired the love of millions of Africans. But in those who worked for him, he inspired a hatred mixed with respect: "He's a strong guy, the kind who could break us." Perhaps that's what love is in Africa. Fela, the great Nigerian artist who opened the door to a new kind of music, was also a very tough man, capable of paying his tour musicians in pennies yet propounding generous ideas. *Djinja:* Africa has the hardness of a stone.

Brussels comforted me. In the last months of 1960, I tried to connect with other Africans. I rubbed shoulders with people who would become the administrators of the post-independence period, while maintaining a semblance of familial authority by hosting my brother and his friends who came for training. From then on, my sights were set on Africa. I felt the need to be thought well of back home; being well known in Brussels and unknown in Cameroon was intolerable to me. I needed to feel comfortable as an African before embarking on an international career. But I was not there yet. I had to know who I was before I could know where I was going. Without realizing it, I did all I could to bring me closer to Cameroon. I foolishly wanted to prove to my parents that I was headed somewhere—this was the battle life had imposed on me. I became deaf to all else, everyone else, every word—except the one that would take me back to Africa.

African Jazz

THE GREAT KABASELE OPENED the gates to paradise for me. He gave me my lucky break, the fabulous offer that altered the course of my life. Decca had just ordered forty recordings from Kabasele—and he wanted me to be his saxophonist.

His band was divided on the question; some feared what I would bring: "Sure, he plays well, but he'll change our music too much." Kabasele talked about the need to be open and fought for me to join African Jazz. In the end, he was the boss; he was loaded, and his wishes were commands. Thanks to a whim of his, a Cameroonian played in his Congolese band, though hardly anyone knew me in Africa, where I had received only a brief mention in the magazine *Bingo*. Subtle bargaining finally resolved the negotiations. I would play sax and sometimes piano.

We recorded about forty songs in two weeks—I who had never set foot in a studio before and had dreamed of doing so one day. This rapid promotion gave me vertigo. Ours was the first joint meeting of Africans on European soil. The technical means at our disposal were on the cutting edge. These records were of exceptional sound quality, although the work was exhausting.

Kabasele Style

As soon as the Anges Noirs closed at five in the morning, I would run to wash up and eat something. Then I was ready for the studio at nine. I recruited replacements for my tea dances. Pepito was the most loyal of all of them. He was Cuban and headed a local band in a neighboring club. He played so beautifully that we were in love with each other. I managed to get him involved in African Jazz. Together we helped create the strange beast that ultimately became the first African music of reference.

Everyone in the band was a star. Each was already well known in the Congo through his widely distributed records. Kabasele was a fantastic singer; Edo Clari, a renowned clarinetist; Docteur Nico, the finest guitarist of the sixties in Africa. Everyone composed, and each brought his compositions to the band. Like a mother watching over her brood, Kabasele purchased these songs from the musicians. The concept of author's rights was at that time virtually unknown, to the greater profit of the Greek and Lebanese businessmen who had settled in Léopoldville.

The two weeks of recording were very rough. While Pepito and I were used to reading sheet music, the Zaireans played by instinct. As soon as we finished a rehearsal, we would start recording. The work was done in a very disorderly way, yet it held up. More than half the songs did not exist before we entered the studio—at whatever hour that happened, African time. Pepito and I would be at the studio at eight, warming up our instruments and fighting off drowsiness. Sessions were supposed to start at nine. The African Jazz clowns would casually arrive at eleven, after a nice long sleep! We became very upset and thought they were making fun of us. The technicians panicked; the producer clearly couldn't have cared less.

Sofrason, Decca's affiliate, owned the whole network—the business end of the music and the pressing plant in Kinshasa. Zaire hummed to the single beat of music and politics. Everything was worked out in the bars. Stars were an integral part of public life. This nation was exceptional in Africa; everywhere else on the continent musicians were nothing less than beggars: "Have a good time, but stay in your place."

By 1989, African artists in Africa would have a hard time making a living from their music. But the Zaireans of 1960 didn't have that problem—they were the pioneers. Kabasele had a gleaming Cadillac and a superb villa in the residential section of Kinshasa, and no one said anything about it. Elsewhere he would have incited jealousy and envy to the point that he would have denied himself such luxury.

Having fifteen songs ready at the start of our studio engagement meant nothing. There was work to be done: we had to record forty. African Jazz could take the heat. One or another of the composers would go off into the stairwell and lay a song, text and tune complete. Egg in hand, he would call the singer-accompanist. Poof! he would pull it all together and copy down the words. Ever onward for the music! Three-quarters of our songs were composed in this way. Then came the guitar and bass. We rehearsed; it flowed. We found the groove right away. The composer would tell us our parts; we wrote them down to save time. And then it was over. I would normally rework a song for at least two hours; at the rate of three or four a day, we completed our order in two weeks. Inventing live like this fascinated me. This method would be lost in the following decades, with the decline of 78s and the rise of 45s. Some of our creations are still on 78s pressed in Kinshasa. The masters didn't always arrive in one piece; oh well . . .

I developed deep ties to Kabasele, the first African producer to work on orders of Sofrason's owner, who himself was a godfather to me. It appears that he was dipping into arms sales to South Africa. People will talk. . . He finally went bankrupt.

The records immediately became more than a local success. All of Africa was captivated; one of the pieces on which I played piano became a favorite Zairean refrain. Without setting foot back on its soil, I became an overnight star in Africa. Thanks to African Jazz, my name began to spread. The fans remembered it. African Jazz also negotiated my engagement with Sofrason. To the band members, I was a phenomenon: no other African could play piano like I could. They liked me and paid me well. When they came to play in Brussels, they dropped off my press clippings. I was swimmingly happy.

Zaire had what it takes to be the leading country as far as music is concerned: a language spoken by many; thirty million fans; an export infrastructure extending throughout the continent. Its products were not targeted to Europe. Kabasele profited admirably from these market characteristics. His Pan-African appeal never overshadowed the musicians who played with him. Each had his share of glory; fame's paradise was open to all.

To fully enter Eden, however, I had to realize a dream that was haunting me: getting my name on a record jacket. Oddly enough, it was this group of Africans who gave me the chance. Kabasele agreed to sponsor me. With my first contract in hand and the godsend of working with Pepito, I made my first record, *African Soul*. Mainly instrumental, it was a flop. Singers liked me as an instrumentalist, but I had no identity yet.

African Soul: From Jazz to Rumba

African Soul was a mixture of jazz, popular music, and rumba. On some songs I sang in Spanish, as I had started to do at the Anges Noirs. I recorded mambos, cha-chas, Latin jazz crossbred with African—"Spanish Harlem," you might say. I called on the best saxophonists, trumpet players, and pianists, all well-known artists that I respected. People I had never even dared to phone before sat in on sessions for me. The orchestration on that album was close to Charlie Parker and to Tito Puente. These arrangements satisfied my deepest desires as well as my concept of music at the time. The recording quality was astounding. Never in Paris could I have had access to such riches—thank you, Zairean independence and Belgium!

I even sang a blues number, "Ecoute, Mon Chéri" ["Listen, My Darling"]. This song was by Roy Floridge, a trumpet player who wrote in a kind of Americanized French: "Listen, my darling, what's the matter with you? / I gave you all my money and you didn't love me. . . / You said you loved me / My love, I don't believe you / My honey, my honey, I'm mad at you / because I'm sick of giving you my money and my love too." The song got me into trouble in Cameroon; Jesuits in Douala denounced me for broadcasting pornography over the radio.

If I was almost a star in Africa, I was merely a musician in Brussels, where I still lived. So I contacted a bunch of producers, but no one wanted anything to do with me. Aiee! Still, I was the only one of all my musician friends to have cut my first record. Audacious and naive, I was crazed because I couldn't bring out records in Brussels under my own name; Adamo himself had to become a Paris exile before he became known. My music had no personality, but I didn't know it then. This was a choice moment for Kabasele to give me a second chance, as he did one luminous day in spring 1961.

African Jazz, Reprise

Kabasele never neglected his business interests. Our recordings together had been successful. In Kinshasa, people were asking about me: "Who's Manu?" This burgeoning interest did not escape our leader, and he invited me to tour for a month in Zaire. Not a bad move given the competition—Franco and his band, OK Jazz, who were less sophisticated and had more popular appeal than African Jazz. And Rochereau—a.k.a. Tabu Ley, the famous singer—had just joined Kabasele's band.

The political situation was changing. The news broadcast clips of blue-helmeted police on the scene to ensure a certain level of civic peace. In my naïveté I imagined that the tour would be problem-free. In any case, it would only last a month. My departure drew me like a magnet, like a siren's song—playing with the stars, maybe I would become one?

The bargaining became more precise throughout the spring and edged toward an agreement for a tour in August. The Anges Noirs would again be closed then. Kabasele offered us a good fee. He purchased the most powerful instruments on the market—trumpets, guitars, amplifiers—and costumes. He called photographers together for the send-off of our equipment by plane. As the bandleader, he had to pay for this material, even if it meant paying the musicians a pittance later on. Kabasele upheld his end with great pomp. Sofrason advanced him the money he needed from his immense royalties previously accrued.

It was a very beautiful spring. Negotiations progressed. Kabasele came back to Brussels. This time he brought Franco and his band. Kabasele had figured out how to negotiate with his European partners; Franco, timid and gifted, didn't know how to yet. In Africa, each man had his fans, as in soccer. The artistic life of Zaire rested entirely on their shoulders. They were both seen as modern because they were the first to introduce electric guitars; they spoke the same language—but they had different ideas. They were enemies and brothers at the same time. Kabasele, with great cleverness, preferred profiting from Franco to obstructing his path. So Franco came to Brussels, a signed contract with Kabasele in hand.

They remained competitors and let everyone know it. To each his club, his band, and his groupies, the spoils to the one with the best instruments. We sensed immediately that there were two teams, two ways of seeing things. My preference lay with Kabasele, a humanist who was open to others. Franco didn't like foreigners coming to Zaire and had a murky relationship with the powers that were. Kabasele really knew how to entice and enchant his entourage.

I would eventually lose a lot of money with Kabasele, the first advance always being the last. In 1967, despite my disappointments,

I formed a band with him and Don Gonzalo, a Cuban who played fantastic flute. It was called African Team—that is, African Jazz, reprise.

On trips to Brussels, members of the musical world sometimes trafficked in diamonds. Coco and I were so naive. Northern Zaire produced industrial diamonds that could practically be obtained on the street. Musicians' suitcases were stuffed with them. We watched fortunes pass before our eyes, never touching them. In the future I would reproach myself for this. A little like my father, I have no predisposition to dishonesty.

Coco, much sharper than I, protected me. She knew my Zairean trip promised ups and downs. We decided not to separate; she joined me in my African adventure. She was hurting, for I no longer heeded her advice and warnings. Clearly I had lost all reason. She guessed at the difficulties that lay ahead for a mixed couple in Africa, and she tried to reason with me. She was not convinced that it was in my interest to go, and she thought my career should be international. But I only had eyes for Africa. I had rubbed shoulders with the leaders of the independence movement, which had only narrowed my sights further.

I was part of the scenery, not an actor in history. History is usually written by men of letters or civil servants; I saw it with my musician's eyes. I was very frustrated not to hear my record on Belgian radio. I compared our African history to that of American jazzmen. Some friends went to study in the United States and returned with records and magazines. They were warmly received in New York because they were African. Black Americans envied their independence, though the debate was complicated, weighed down by four centuries of slavery. Our ancestors had sold people to the whites—two hundred million slaves. Black Americans have not completely forgiven us.

At the end of July 1961, we packed our bags for the Brussels–Kinshasa flight and a month-long tour with Kabasele.

The Tam-Tam
of Léopoldville

ZAIRE—AFRICAN PARADISE. At this point, the capital still bore its quaint colonial name: Léopoldville. Kinshasa would emerge from the sound and fury of civil war with the beauty of a New York in miniature. Homes were made of marble; hotels were comfortable. The colonialists had built an ultramodern metropolis to last an eternity. I had dreamed of an Africa that looked like this. She welcomed me—wealthy, flashy. The transition was an easy one. Accompanied by Kabasele, the brilliant event-maker known as "Le Grand Kallé," I became an event myself. A clever businessman, Kabasele dragged me around with him everywhere. From the first night, he put Coco and me up in his sumptuous villa. The tour started immediately. African Jazz played for dignitaries—Kasavubu and company. I wanted very much to call on the brother of Patrice Lumumba, who had just been assassinated.

The air was sensually moist. Money, sex, sorcery, and physical strength combined in this capital, which was creating its own language and building its own history. At dusk, when candles and gas lamps were lit in the Cité—the black side of town—the crowds would surge, warm and talkative. In the *ngandas*, the many open-air bars, women and men sat in front of the cases of beer that surrounded the stage. The great Kabasele and his African Jazz called forth the crowd's madness—undulating bodies, hot glances, soft eyes, fast talk, and the hips of beautiful dancers held in their skin-tight wrappers. Pale beers were gulped down between two plates of fish served with plantain or manioc—*la dolce vita*. One night the band left the Cité's enchantments to play an evening party in the provinces. We took a plane. The control tower was often deserted, so a schoolteacher, the only remaining Belgian, would transmit instructions from the tower to the pilot—which didn't stop him from landing in the trees sometimes, from landing anywhere at all. Here, pilots were a little vague about their job. Luck often took the place of a license.

As I embarked on an African life-style, I lost no time succumbing to its fun-house mirrors, and reality lost no time catching up with me. One week after our arrival, Kabasele's villa was burglarized; all of our bags disappeared. Having lost face, the Zaireans became all the more zealous about trying to find the thief. He was quickly arrested but admitted to having sold everything off already. A strange atmosphere reigned in the residential district where we lived. Not long ago, the Belgians had demanded a pass to go beyond the border between the Ville (the white section) and the Cité. Now the police drove along the broad avenues without stopping. The Europeans had fled.

Mixed marriages were not in fashion. I almost stopped going out so as not to leave Coco alone. Fat-cat military men stopped me and offered to buy my wife—after all, I was just a musician. Why shouldn't they have Coco? The band members themselves asked strange questions: Why have just one wife and not several "offices" (that is, mistresses)? Coco confronted this unknown environment— with not even the shadow of a white person—as I had long ago in the Sarthe region, where I had gone months without seeing a single black person. Having only one wife also made me a rare bird. And I was not the same kind of musician they were, either. Who was I to talk to? Beyond music, we had no common ground. We didn't have the same cultural "baggage" or the same habits. My relationship with Coco had its own rhythm.

At Kabasele's, the spontaneous comings and goings never stopped. Talking about music was not enough, but Belgian political instruction was clearly not intended to create intellectuals in its Congo. A real rift formed between us and the other musicians. We didn't belong to the same collective memory. I wanted to know everything, and my mental life began to show it. I had trouble functioning without my past. Accustomed to passionate discussions over quiet dinners at home, I forced myself to go out with the guys and wander the Cité. It was in those bars that "business" was transacted.

Despite all common sense, I fell in love with Africa. I began to learn about her—at a high price. This first lesson would last my whole life, all my stays on the continent. The numerous difficulties I was faced with didn't quench my thirst. I was infatuated, and my only desire was to move to Zaire permanently. Against its landscape I was a very particular black man, but at least I fit the decor. In this class-stratified society, which demanded to know immediately the rank of its guests, I was a mere musician, a social zero. Yet I was seen everywhere. I wanted to prove that making music *was* a profession. I had left for a month but decided to prolong my stay in Zaire—for two years, which proved to be as crazy as they were rough.

Coco was bored. She spent her afternoons at the pool of a fancy hotel, where she met her compatriots. We became friendly with its French owner. He organized sophisticated parties amid the luxuriant foliage of his garden and hired a Zairean band with whom I played on occasion. I especially liked to jam with the Dutch and the Belgians staying at the hotel. It filled a need in me; with Le Grand Kallé, we played only in the Cité. At the Juan-les-Pins club happily I met up once more with Vicky Down, whom I knew from Brussels. He had just signed a contract with Sabena Airlines and moved to Léopoldville with his wife, also a music lover. At last I had a little group beyond African Jazz with whom I could think and talk!

Wily Kabasele had clearly understood it all. When the tour ended, he casually suggested to me, "I have a nightclub, the Afro-Négro on Avenue du Général de Gaulle. Since you don't want to play with us anymore . . ." The man had seen us running around in search of people to meet, in search of jazz and Western culture. He moved heaven and earth so Coco and I could take over the Afro-Négro. He wanted me to start a house band there. I accepted enthusiastically.

I was happy to be settled at home again, even though it did make me terribly angry sometimes. I violently rejected the Rousseauvian image of Africa that haunted the brains of so many patriots. Africans seemed to be paralyzed by the future. They didn't seem to believe in tomorrow, and their only concern was to fill the present moment as well as possible. Fatalism had become second nature: "The world is as it is, we're not even its fleas." Today I still think sometimes that Africa has lost her pride. She has fallen into a deep sleep, and when she awakens, her various Princes Charming will look like ogres. The system devours its children and the rest of the planet watches the show, telling itself that though something's rotten in the black kingdom, there's no need to change what seems eternal. The misunderstanding is profound. Already, in Léopoldville, I had guessed at its origins. But the Afro-Négro drew me into its net, entranced me.

"Twist à Léo"

We started at the Afro-Négro in October. I organized the band, and Coco ran the club. Our success was electrifying. With its location right downtown, the UN functionaries loved it, and so did all of the hip Europeans looking for something new. Jazz, salsa, popular music, and the menu—a novelty here—attracted the clientele. Coco sang with the band and took care of the ordering, the food, and the artists' fees. Pulling it all together was a miracle. My wife handled it with great aplomb. We made lots of money—too much, in fact: the national currency, the zaire, was worthless outside the country, and Zairean stores were devoid of "exotic" items from Europe.

Once a week we would dash to the port, where we exchanged our local bills for CFA francs. We then ran to the ferry, which arrived in Brazzaville twenty minutes later. There awaited a mini-paradise: all of us expatriates at the supermarket buying piles of foreign cheeses. This was our blessed day to go to "civilization," and we awaited it impatiently. Each time the shuttle departed, a massive pushing and shoving for a seat ensued on this ferry of Ali Baba promises. The merchants' petty arguments sounded like soccer matches. When we were ready to return, the Brazzaville port would be overflowing with bags, live poultry, mechanical parts, and bottles filled with precious substances. The wharf was crawling with kids hanging onto their mothers' skirts, men loaded down like donkeys, Europeans slapping away mosquitoes greedy for white skin—a joyful brouhaha in homage to Brazzaville. When, by unfortunate happenstance, the ferry didn't go out that day—because of a tiff between the presidents of the two Congos, or because a musician amused himself taking some dignitary's favorite "office" in one capital or the other—it was devastating.

Transferring money was the real problem. We joked about it with other "Westerners": "So, how are *your* transfers going?" But it was not our main subject of concern. Despite influential friends, we could not find a place to live. We moved from one apartment to the next, each loaned to us for a month or two. We couldn't live in a hotel all year. There was no question of moving to the Cité—the mentality there was too different, and I was responsible for Coco. In two years, we found no house to rent long-term. It was very tough.

During this period, many Zaireans were squatting houses owned by organizations or by Europeans. Authorities in the newly independent country did not necessarily have the ability to expel them. The squatters had the use of these buildings without their maintenance. It was the end of an era; the vestiges of past splendor deteriorated very quickly. But we got by in style. We survived, gradually transferring our earnings with the help of American, Belgian, or French connections.

We managed the Afro-Négro for a year, until our relationship with Le Grand Kallé began to falter. He didn't always keep his word; the smallest detail meant we had to race against the clock to pick up the slack. Such was the strength of African inertia. The breakup was smooth. We had just met Dokolo, a wealthy banker living in a luxurious villa facing the town hall. He had heard me play at the Afro-Négro and suggested that we start a new club. So we created the Tam-Tam, our first club.

We changed neighborhoods. I kept my band. It was all very complicated. The instruments we had purchased on the street often broke. My guitarist had a knack for surprising me: on Saturday nights, when the Tam-Tam was jammed, he would come running in to say, "Oh, boss, my strings are broken!" I put in a huge piano. That was a draw: pianos were rare in Africa because they don't take the climate well. I pushed my musicians hard. I made them go beyond what they knew. They had to play my standards in the latest style. I had records sent by the boxload from the United States, Belgium, and France: the freshest jazz, Stevie Wonder's first hits, and so on. Then I arranged them according to my taste.

The Tam-Tam had an odd charm. The spirit here was different from that in other nightly meeting places. The decor certainly wasn't extravagant. Every evening was a party, and the public crowded in. Sometimes we even refused customers for lack of space. Now that I had my own business, my quarrel with the musical world ended. I could play with whomever I wanted; I could go to whichever side of town I wanted. I finally began composing. The twist had just invaded Kinshasa. The record stores had few foreign recordings in their racks. At the end of 1961, all you could find was Tino Rossi's "Petit Papa Noel" ["Little Father Christmas"]. All of a sudden, Bob Azzam's hit "Amen Twist" burst onto the scene like a bomb. The wave washed over the Tam-Tam; customers asked for it over and over again. I didn't know any other twists, so I thought for a while . . . it was just a blues rock. So I made one up. My first twist

was called "Twist à Léo" ["Twist in Léopoldville"]. From Limete to
Kalina, the song spanned the fifty miles from one end of the city to
the other. In the song I talked about a neighborhood, part of the
Cité, putting words everyone understood to a rhythm that had nothing African about it. Hip young Kinshasans called for the twist. My
song was about their turf and became their twist. From one end of
Zaire to the other, the news traveled: "Can you believe it? They're
dancing the twist in Léopoldville!" In a word, a Congo twist! I became enmeshed in the pop music machine. I had the notion to start
the song with "Ah-eh, ah-eh, ah-eh," and everybody sang along
with it.

This launched me as a modern music maker. In the first quarter
of 1962 I left for Brussels, where Sofrason, via Kallé, had ordered a
series of 45s, among them "Twist à Léo." For the occasion, I again
worked with Le Grand Kallé and collaborated with African Jazz,
with its same strong team spirit. The record was a triumph. "Twist
à Léo" inundated Africa. For obscure logistical reasons, I put out a
second version in Cameroon later. I admit I lost a lot of money with
Kabasele, but on the other hand, he gave me the keys to all the
kingdoms I wanted to enter.

I returned to Kinshasa and again took up the reins at the Tam-
Tam. Each to his own devices.

"Mami Wata"

Zaire's flashy lights began to dim. Music, girls, beer, buddies—the
easy life left me a little cold. Over the months I discovered other
crowds. The Cité's thousand lights no longer dazzled me; I would
go there for entertainment, as I would to a soccer match. I joined
mozikis—groups bound by affinity but not by secrets. Each moziki
has its own friends and rules. An event that takes place in the life of
one of its members becomes common property. Mozikis are a vital
part of daily life. This kind of group exists throughout Africa, sometimes enriched by tontines who finance their business projects. As a
foreigner in Kinshasa, I was content to be an honorary member of
several mozikis. The gods were not dead in Zaire.

I thought about bringing my parents to visit us. I had an ulterior
motive; I was calculating. My parents didn't know my wife. Coming
here, they would meet her on neutral ground, far from the pressures
and weight of family life. I wrote to them. Euphoria! Douala instantly learned the news. They so badly needed to talk about it: "No,

he's not a doctor, but he's flying both of us . . ." One April morning in 1962 they took a plane to Pointe-Noire, going by train from there to Brazzaville, where they had relatives. We met them there, and they met Coco. My mother couldn't speak French, but she understood it. Responding as a woman, she thought my wife was very beautiful. My father was happy to get to know Kinshasa. Each of us was happy for different reasons; what joy to see each other again! We carefully avoided talking about the essential thing. Coco did all she could to ensure that everything went off without a hitch. Cut off from their daily habits, my parents loved my wife. I handled the necessary translations.

To my parents, the Zairean capital looked like a black Paris. The success of the Tam-Tam, filled with foreigners and expatriates, calmed them down about how I was doing. Plane tickets paid for, a full cashbox—they were proud. I put them up at the lovely Memling Hotel. I went to such lengths to try to change their minds that I almost went overboard. As my mother grew closer to Coco, my father had his own ideas. Since I had convinced him that music was a profession, that I could make big money, he thought about it, weighed the pros and cons, and wound up asking me, "Why don't you come to Cameroon and do what you're doing here?"

"Mami Wata," the Cameroonian sirens' song, started playing. My somber stopover in Douala two years ago—forgotten! My father countered all my objections. He was clear: "The situation is much better now; the curfew is over." In fact, he had come to Kinshasa to convince me that everything was different back home. I insisted on going with my wife. My parents had a deep affection for her, while regretting that she was not Cameroonian—fear of the foreigner, once again. They avoided talking about it; we skirted the problem. The connection remained fragile. But on this point I felt I must confront reality. Back home, marrying a woman from another ethnic group was no easy matter; my parents should know. My situation was even more delicate—Coco was white. I was in luck since they liked her; it was balm to my heart. But sentiment would not suffice. This mixed marriage naturally remained a thorny issue. Returning would require melting into society all over again. Otherwise the danger could be great—just like Nyoungou, the maleficent genie that everyone talks about but never sees.

My parents convinced me to return to Cameroon, and I managed to convince Coco. I had told her so much about my country. "You've already seen Kinshasa—home is just like this . . ." A fool's vision. The Zairean capital, the Europeans' royal path in Africa, would make Douala look like a provincial garrison. So much I didn't say! I thought only of my own plans. At the Tam-Tam, I had only handled the music. If my future club took off, it would be a business on which to base ambitious enterprises. Starting a club was not an end in itself. I tried to take some of my musicians. The Zaireans who made up the band got caught up in the idea. I had taught them the basics of sight-reading and the standards; they liked this atmosphere. Luck had smiled on us. Omnipresent malaria had not managed to devour us, which was lucky since only Brazzaville possessed a little medicine for it. Sure of my "lucky star," I took the plunge. My parents were thrilled. We closed our first Tam-Tam in Kinshasa forever. All aboard for Cameroon.

Neighborhood Business

ON 6 JANUARY 1963, COCO AND I landed in Douala. Another curious journey intersected with ours: Max Kouta of the Douala Regional School, one of the friends I had grown up with, who had been living in Spain, had just died there from an epileptic fit. I hadn't seen him since our crazy lark in San Sebastian in the summer of 1956. Now his body was coming home. I went to the burial. Coco endured disappointment after disappointment: the Douala whose charms I had so hyped existed only in my memories. After Kinshasa, the city looked like a big village to us. The sun hit hard and the humidity stuck to the skin. The beach near Bonanjo was gone. The great fish-pond in the Ngodi section of town had shrunk to the size of a pocket handkerchief. The beach of my childhood games had moved thirty kilometers away; you had to wade through slimy mud to get there. Driving along with Max's funeral procession, I dropped Coco off there. Her desire to swim withstood these unpleasant surprises. She dared to raise her skirt just above her knees. Black passersby couldn't get over it; the rare whites who drove by stopped to make fun of this phenomenon with the incredible blond hair. A show-off, Coco spent the whole afternoon there.

Bad beginnings. The nightmare deepened. My parents' home was spacious but lacked the basic amenities and had no air-conditioning. It was two kilometers to the center of town, and we had to walk because we didn't have a car. The few musicians who had come with me from Zaire stayed in a house nearby to save money. There were no other mixed couples around. My parents were exuberant in their joy, but Coco broke down. I took her to a better-housed friend.

The first vow of my initiation came back to me: fear of the foreigner, interdiction against white women, the heavy responsibility of the "elect." I was the one chosen to carry the whole crowd. What on earth was I doing in Cameroon? First of all, starting a club. I had brought some sophisticated equipment in my bags—an echo chamber and electronic gadgets unheard of here. I had to make a name for myself. In order to do so, I had to perform every day, as I did in Kinshasa. There was no point in thinking any more about returning to Belgium or France; we were prisoners, condemned to go forward. I looked for a place to open my club. The formalities were time-consuming and complicated. My father, who was not a night person, had misinformed me. Curfew did still exist, and all entertainment establishments had to close their doors at the stroke of midnight.

Of course every rule has its exception. My half-brother in the internal revenue service, tried to make my job easier. The regional police chief received me and finally gave me authorization to create my club. Was this the end of my troubles? I quickly realized that my natural naïveté had fooled me.

Mozart

I established the club next to the imposing Jesuits' school. At this point, my plans hardly seemed to upset them. The police had surveyed the neighborhood. Ten minutes away by foot, prostitutes and sailors met regularly in the Mozart neighborhood, as everyone knew. I composed a ballad to it as a kind of dedication. Augustin Black, director of the newly created National Radio, and Jacques Moudiki, one of my music-loving friends, gave me brilliant publicity over the airwaves—such solidarity among the hometown boys. I had invested all the savings I had in my transfer accounts. But before ever opening the club, I lacked the funds to pay my band.

A couple of French friends—an ex-fireman who owned a club and his florist wife—helped me organize three evenings that rocked Douala. The whole thing went down in history. Zillions of kids crowded the palm and avocado trees around the club where we were playing, hanging onto any branch that looked like it would support them since they didn't have the money for a ticket.

At the end of January Coco and I inaugurated our second Tam-Tam. Success was instantaneous. It was the talk of all Douala, and soon all Cameroon. The people had never seen such an atmosphere. The echo chamber amplified our voices (my beautiful blond Coco sang with us). The Tam-Tam was on the cutting edge. Spacious and beautifully decorated, it took up the ground floor of an old home built by the Germans before the First World War. The building was solid and cleverly designed: good ventilation advantageously replaced air-conditioning, which we could not have counted on to function regularly. We lived in an apartment above. The band played only the latest songs. The Tam-Tam's repertoire cut a wholly different groove from the stuff being played in the hotels and clubs of Mozart. Word of mouth expanded our reputation. To Cameroonians, always receptive to the arts, I was like a pioneer, the first to practice music as a profession.

At the Tam-Tam, members of the "cool" set just back from France, encrusted with diplomas, paraded around with their girls. Expatriates made it their favorite nightspot. They and the civil servants became our regulars. My reputation swelled. Bokassa, then commander of the army of the Central African Republic, came frequently by plane from the capital, Bangui. He would spend an insane amount and stay until dawn. His bills went directly to the president of the C.A.R. Women, and again, women! Ministers made the trip over from Yaoundé to kick up their heels at the Tam-Tam. High on my newborn prestige, I dreamed of creating an arts institute, a goal of civic usefulness I had cherished for a long time.

My fall was all the harder. Underhanded schemes against me took place in broad daylight. My troubles accumulated, born of discreet intrigue carried out behind my back. I was utterly surprised, and I wrote a song about it. The Jesuits told the media that I had come to bring debauchery to Douala and that my music incited the viler instincts in the lower belly. I was propagating prostitution in Cameroon, they claimed, because the whores from Mozart all came to the Tam-Tam. Suddenly, one night, the police burst in. The commissioner took me aside, embarrassed. "I love your music," he said. He gave me to understand that I needed a protector; of course I didn't have one. What use was being warned?

The police broke in more and more often. We didn't even have time to breathe anymore. Our customers were dragged to the police station for vexation and verification of their papers, which were not always in order. One evening, at five minutes to twelve, in the presence of a minister friend, the army burst in again, submachine guns at the ready this time. Panic. Rumors grew in Douala: "You can't go to the Tam-Tam anymore. Such strange things happen there, the police . . ." Opinion turned against my Tam-Tam. Funny coincidence: the city created an entertainment tax that drained fifteen percent off everything we took in! We were living in hell. In fact, in Cameroon, in my birthplace, I passed through every circle of hell. The authorities could decorate me with all the medals they liked; the descent into hell continued.

Coco and I felt a very strong atmosphere of hatred around us. Who was feeding this jealousy? We had a hard time imagining, but we ended up understanding the source of all the intrigues. According to the rumor mill of "sidewalk radio," the police chief who had given me authorization to open in the first place had an interest in one of the nightclubs in the neighborhood, which was run by his French mistress. We were her direct competitors. Now we discovered how far the conspiracy spread. But that was not all. Ingenuously, as a man aware of his commitments and respectful of his tradition, I had hired members of my own family to wash dishes, make food, guard, and wait tables. But they were joyfully stealing from me on the sly. Such was the hard reality at home. Coco, knowing how sensitive I was, dared to say nothing. In six months, our funds had been devoured.

"Soir au Village"

I wrote a song about people's daily concerns, "Soir au Village" ["Evening in the Village"]. It reminded me of houses in my childhood and traditional foods. Cameroon was coming to a new phase. The nation was being created, and the authorities didn't have time to fantasize. The opportunity to dream grew smaller and smaller, although people had a strong need for it. The lack was painful to me. In the months that followed, this feeling only worsened. The jealousy Coco and I incited knew no respite. One night while I was sleeping, a deadly minute snake coiled under my pillow. In the morning, one of the houseboys found it while cleaning. It didn't get me. I was still convinced that I was decidedly lucky. It had been set there to kill me—not for the first time. I obsessed on a childhood memory—serpents under my bed. My father's family, of an ethnic group different from my mother's, had not accepted me. Old messages from African mythology sanctioned excluding me, making me go away, killing me. Worse, I had aggravated the problem by leaving the country for fifteen years and bringing back a foreign woman. On later stays in Cameroon, snakes would reappear regularly. In the street one day someone pushed me rudely and I turned around in anger. A snake, nested in a palm tree, was pointing its head toward me. The reptile was going to make its meal of me. These stories cannot be understood by a Western mind but are explicable to Africans. In this harmful atmosphere we painfully closed our fourth month at the Tam-Tam.

The Cameroonian Red Cross, presided over by the minister of health, invited the band to an evening concert at the Municipal Circle of Yaoundé. What great publicity to show off in the capital, where the whole diplomatic corps lived! We were burning with impatience. Taking the train was a gamble. As a precaution, we stored the instruments under the foldout beds. As soon as we arrived, we lost our spirits: President Kennedy had just been assassinated in Dallas and our government had decided to have national mourning for a whole week. A concert was out of the question. The minister of health didn't even receive us. Encumbered by our instruments, penniless, we didn't know how we would eat or where we would sleep—a fine illustration of the brutality inherent in the life of a country. There was no place for emotion. I felt hatred for certain individuals, but not for my country.

Our penury was absolute. We had to get out of this. I ran over to the house of a childhood friend, Missipo Bodjongo, a hospital pharmacist. He hurried to our aid, setting up a discreet meeting with the minister in a quiet corner of the main market. There we had an argument fit for fishwives: "Yes, I hired you. But the president has said there will be no playing." I explained, "We have to return to Douala, and we have no money." He answered that he budgeted no expenditures. Missipo finally found a way out. The musicians stayed at the firehouse. A sum was released for our meals and return tickets. Coco did not appreciate the kind of wheeling and dealing in which we were mired. I took her everywhere with me. She didn't understand the point of this. She told me again, "You're not living in reality."

After we returned to the Tam-Tam, our existence dragged on. As part of Douala's first festival, the Canadian Brothers called on me to open for Gilbert Bécaud's show. The concert was free to the public. What a crowd! When Bécaud went on stage, the audience protested. They wanted to hear me. Already chauvinism marked the moment. My success was in the people's love for me, something that couldn't be bought. Our politicians may have had money, but they certainly didn't have the love of the people. We had what they didn't have, and they let us know it. With such jealousy . . .

The Congolese guys in my band—whom I'd paid and lodged ten times better than they would have found anywhere else, and whom I respected deeply—returned to Kinshasa. I hired Cameroonians. Despite their great reputations, they gave me the biggest headaches, with union obligations as their pretext—as if Cameroon were Europe. In Africa, musicians have a day job and become a club owner's slaves at night. They're hired for a bit of bread, just the length of time it takes some notable to get married to the sounds of traditional music.

That was not how things were done at the Tam-Tam. To everyone's mystification, I closed myself off in a very negative circle. After the sixth month of hell, I had to close up shop, staggering under debt. But I still had one more trick up my sleeve . . .

"Flottez Drapeaux sur Yaoundé"

Dieng, a Senegalese man married to a cousin of my mother's, owned the Black & White in Yaoundé, a club that was doing very well. He had his protectors. He offered me a contract that allowed us to share profits equally. He would invest the capital, and we would run the club. Yaoundé was the administrative and intellectual capital of Cameroon. With nothing left to lose, we decided to move to Yaoundé. We rented a house near the Black & White. The city was full of beautiful valleys. The boss loaned us a huge green Chevrolet that often broke down. After closing, at three in the morning, we had to push the car to get it started. The memory is unforgettable. Our neighbors across the landing, a military family, tried to pick fights with us. But these scraps seemed slight after Douala's somber jealousy.

For the Tropics Soccer Cup, the authorities adopted a hymn composed by yours truly—"Flottez Drapeaux sur Yaoundé" ["May Flags Fly over Yaoundé"]. I recorded my songs, interwoven with threads of daily life, for the radio. My genre was the blues, a fairly standard introduction with hybrid harmonies, jazz, and Latin—not the style in fashion in Africa, but pleasing to the smart crowd at the Black & White. Coco and I were favorites of the diplomatic clientele. But I soon started to get bored. We would go to the movies on our days off, but I had no music to listen to. We could only hear traditional music in the city. Every night, until five in the morning, every neighborhood had its own tam-tams playing. People danced. These evening sounds mixed with the chirping of the crickets. Sometimes I could hear a veritable four-part harmony.

I didn't lack opportunities to play outside Yaoundé in the countries surrounding Cameroon. Lion's Clubs and Rotary Clubs regularly hosted me and the band. Incredible flights on shaky DC-4s . . . These escapades did not fill my need for a musical milieu. Coco weakened and fell seriously ill. Her father had just died in Belgium, and I couldn't give her a plane ticket. She took care of herself as best she could without medicines and appropriate care.

"Répondez-Nous, Seigneur"

We suffocated more and more in the climate of suspicion that reigned in the capital. Everyone saw the neighbors as potential stool pigeons. Everyone talked in cautious whispers. Everyone was wary of everyone else. In the shadow of colonialism, African life remained regulated, anchored to its familial model. With independence attained, Cameroon was in search of unity, but the transition dismantled the balance that already existed. Citizens of many different ethnic groups were foreigners to one another: lost in the capital, they didn't know one another. Nor did planners think it a priority to build roads connecting people. They also refused to give themselves the gift of a national television station—such a costly tool. Apparently there was no money to create programs. It seemed impossible to master this tool. Politicians were afraid of it. They preferred to ruin the country by prestige-seeking operations—the production of cocoa and coffee that had been planted by the colonialists and was sold at a low rate on the world market. That did not prevent the building of useless palaces. The country lived according to a foreign model beyond its means. Its only ambition was to take advantage of the model and profit from it. The country's leaders had no other example and little imagination.

Once an indigenous African civilization existed. By taking the trouble, we could find its trail, thanks to oral tradition. But who will make the effort? No doubt, Africa has had a bad break in its history. Since then, it is incapable of thinking of others and of its own future. Yet creating anew is the only path to health. The opportunities exist, though they arouse only disdain. Africa's wealth is its creativity: it is our "real" coffee, our "real" cocoa. Africa treats its ills so casually. It waits for rich countries to erase its debt. This is a cheat of a remedy: the people and their successive governments tell themselves it will always be this way. Both lose in this illusion, to the point of forgetting the few vestiges of the culture they had. The statues die, too.

"Répondez-nous, Seigneur" ["Answer us, Lord"], John William sang on the record I had just bought. This mixed-race black singer, a Frenchman, was certainly a product of his time. Upset, uprooted, disappointed, Coco and I couldn't go on any longer.

"Nasengina"

"Luck" appeared once again. One bright day in 1964, the mayor of Santa Isabel Malabo—a tiny island under Spanish control in the Gulf of Guinea—telephoned to invite me to a week-long cultural festival he was organizing. I had known him a long time, and he liked my music. This was the first time he had brought a French-speaking African band to his island. The DC-3 that took us to the airport right at the water's edge barely managed to avoid a nosedive. The welcoming ceremony was fantastic. Santa Isabel, which had still not experienced the horrors of dictatorship, had the charm of a Spanish town, with a cathedral, a very beautiful square that looks like the Alhambra, and beautiful cultivated coffee fields. We were hooked.

Iberia, the airline serving Santa Isabel, continued on to Europe for a price that beat all the competition. We had a thought: "What if we went back to Europe? We should save up some money, then open an account in Paris that we could use if need be . . ." I got brave. Our hosts paid us a royal sum. I asked them to set aside a part of it for two plane tickets that they would keep safe. Then we returned to Cameroon, where work picked up again. I composed "Nasengina," my only piece constructed purely from the indigenous Cameroonian makossa. "Nasengina" would later be covered by a Caribbean group.

Time passed. What to do with our oh-so-reassuring plane tickets? We didn't know where to go in Europe. I suggested returning to Brussels. The Anges Noirs was still going: I could get a return engagement there. My wife refused: "We should go to Paris." I thought about our security. Coco was looking farther ahead: "In Paris, opportunities to play are endless." "I don't know anyone in the business there," I retorted. We discussed it for a long time. Finally, I wrote to a childhood friend I had made in France. Jean was the son of one of the richest men in Cameroon. As teens and then as young men, we had had some good times together. In 1956, he had managed to convince the owner of a tennis club in San Sebastian to allow us in by bragging about his "superb black band." A deal was struck. Jean, whom we had nicknamed "Juanito" because of his passion for Cuban music, played the tumbas. We stayed in a bullfighter's villa. Juanito had planned to have us play in Palma de Mallorca afterward. But he never came to the gig, and we found ourselves without a dime, knowing no one. His supposed contacts affirmed that they had never heard of the whole deal. That summer we had to play in the streets—me on sax, Francis Kingué dancing, and Benn's Ndiné on tam-tams.

Juanito hadn't forgotten a thing. Memories, memories. He answered the letter I sent from Yaoundé right away. Spring 1964 passed slowly. Finally, Jean sent me a copy of the contract he had snagged in Spain. We had one season to get afloat again, and then we could establish ourselves in Paris. No sooner said than done. The owner of the Black & White was not happy. My mother, who often came to stay with us, guessed nothing. I simply told my parents that Coco had to visit her family after her father's death and that we were taking the opportunity to go on vacation, since she was exhausted.

At the end of June, we sneaked out of Cameroon.

Soul Party

JUANITO WAS AWAITING US IN PARIS. Newly married, he had a Latin passion for his Spanish wife, who came from a well-known family. Unfortunately, he couldn't host us at their home, and we had to settle in at the Hôtel de France, a lovely place near the Ecole Militaire. Between restaurant meals and nights at the hotel, our savings would barely last a month. As for the season's contract we signed, it evaporated—Spanish castles in the air. Anxiety gripped us anew. Our few friends were students. I was a complete unknown in the jazz milieu. So I sat in on vibraphone or sax, just to prove I existed as a musician. One swallow didn't make it springtime—I was doing nothing to build our future.

Kuadjo, our Ivoirian buddy, entered into the game and saved us. It was June, and he was in Paris for President Houphouët-Boigny's son's wedding. The prestigious ceremony was planned for the Hôtel Crillon, on the Place de la Concorde, under the gaze of everyone who was anyone in Paris, plus African dignitaries. Kuadjo had been asked to pull together a band for the occasion, and he brought me into it. We rehearsed feverishly. They loved our performance. The fee allowed Coco and me to improve our standard of living. And the band survived beyond the presidential event.

Our angel Kuadjo, who lived in Bouake, where he ran a fabric mill, had married a Breton woman. He was crazy about Saint-Cast in Saint-Brieuc Bay, where his in-laws resided. He spent every vacation there. Moved by our troubles, he said, "Nothing doing this summer? I'll find you something." And all we had to do was agree.

Our man went off in his Simca over the Brittany roads to scout for
a week. He was the king of deals. Known in the area, he succeeded
in convincing the owner of The Casino in Saint-Cast to take us on.
The man wanted nothing to do with a band and didn't have the
money to pay for one. Kuadjo managed to bring him around: "It
won't cost a thing. You can pay them on a percentage basis." "OK,"
the guy said, "if I don't have any expenses." On his return to Paris,
our friend gave us the good news without keeping the hard part from
us: "The Casino can't put you up. A lot of young jet-setters go there;
give them some New Orleans–style tunes, and they'll flock to the
club. Be brave, and the percentage will follow."

Kuadjo was a fighter. His excitement was infectious—the kind
of person you'd like to meet more often in life. His generosity was
limitless, and we had just about hit bottom. The guy had thought
of everything. He had already rented a big villa to house the six
musicians of the band and their wives. Kuadjo just told us modestly,
"I'll advance you the money you need for a deposit and the first
month's rent, something to eat, and a little pocket money. We'll
settle the rest later." He approached divinity. At the wheel of his
Simca, he made four Paris–Brittany trips, over a thousand kilometers each time, without even taking the time to sleep. He transported
all our equipment—the drums, Yves Beugré's guitar, Jeannot "Karl"
Dikoto's double bass tied to the roof, and tenor and soprano saxes
(in memory of Sidney Bechet).

We arrived in Saint-Cast one early morning in July.

Sidney Bechet's Cousin

The Casino's owner was overflowing with kindness. He had announced the arrival of our band through several ads in the *Ouest-
France*, the regional daily. I played "Les Oignons," "Petite
Fleur"—Sidney Bechet's hits. A journalist wrote, with flowery prose,
that I was "Sidney Bechet's cousin." A young band for a young
crowd. The Casino was always stuffed to the gills. The initial month-
long contract was extended to August. Life flowed serenely on,
though we were hardly rolling in money. We nonetheless managed
to set some aside. Our wives helped us behind the scenes. At our
urging, Coco and her friend Françoise, the wife of Benn, the drummer, gave in to a little fancy-cheese trafficking at the nearby supermarket: a quick switch of labels, and a great meal was had at a low
price. We were a real family, all together in this villa by the sea.

August ended along with the contract. The Casino's owner urged me to stay. He had fallen in love with the talents of fifteen-year-old Micheline Bouvier, who imitated Piaf in the most exquisite fashion. She added the songs of Jean Ferrat to her repertoire, accompanying herself on the accordion. She was Brittany's own phenomenon. Her admirer served as her impresario. He wanted to make her a star and wanted me to accompany her in future shows. My friends in the band, who lived in Paris full-time, returned home. But I had nothing to do in the capital. I didn't even have a house. Why not stay on in Saint-Cast?

The Casino's boss found a piano and a villa Coco liked: wood fires in the chimney as the moon rose. I wandered around on long walks across the deserted beaches where the mist turned to fine rain. In the afternoon I rehearsed with Micheline. We had a few nibbles—a contract opening for Sacha Distel, a recording contract with a Paris company. I composed a song for Micheline with words by Leroy, a printer connected to our Saint-Cast sponsor. We spent a month getting the 45 ready; its B-side was a Piaf song. The like of my work with Micheline has never been seen, before or since—a big black man behind a fragile young white woman. Early in October, I left for Paris, promising to return to Brittany for every contract she had.

Coco and I moved into a studio apartment on Rue Roger, near the big open-air market along Rue Daguerre. The few square meters allowed us space for a bed, my vibraphone, and the sax. The toilet was on the landing. But at last we had a roof over our heads. Our window opened onto the strange cemetery in Montparnasse. Nights were spent wandering from one jazz club to another. One thing led to the next, and I learned that every Tuesday at Place Pigalle musicians in need of work gathered at a job center. From six to eight, bandleaders looking for musicians would go there. "I have a dance six blocks away; I need a saxophonist who can play a second instrument during the tangos. I hear you play sax. Can you also play a little bass or piano or organ?" Each Thursday, a similar gathering took place in front of the Théâtre de la Renaissance. Throughout the fall of 1965, I kept these dates faithfully.

At the same time, I often went to the Bohème, a nightclub on Rue d'Odessa, near Montparnasse Station, run by the astonishing Tony, a Yugoslav. The man had played every American base in France from here to hell and back again since the Liberation. He was quite familiar with the traffic in cigarettes so popular now. He had genius. His Bohème brought in avant-garde bands playing newly imported rhythm and blues. The ambiance attracted lots of black American soldiers going off base for an evening's fun. I came in with my sax and made contact with this one and that. With the help of a Caribbean baritone sax player, I met Rocky Cortes, who led a dance band. Also of Yugoslavian origin, he lived in Nanterre and had taken a Latin-sounding professional name. His trademark was hiring only blacks, preferably Caribbean or African. His was the only black band to play the dance-hall circuit in France. (He would later become Claude François's chauffeur.)

Now he was staggering under offers to play at dances. His bravado seduced me: I responded with my own when he asked if I could play organ. Without the least hesitation I said, "Yes!" No scruples here. The band played just a little salsa, but its black image masked its inadequacies. Rocky played only clubs in the tiniest towns, abandoned by more famous performers such as Aimable or Verchuren. In the countryside, Saturday-night dances were an important tradition. I played for Rocky across thousands of kilometers and in all kinds of weather, trying my hand at the organ, never telling him my secret. When I returned from these escapades, I had time to hang out in the jazz clubs. I sat in at the Trois Maillets, the Chat Qui Pêche, and the Caméléon.

People started to know me. At the Bohème I met Michel Boss, an excellent French trumpet player, a solid friend who always had a funny story. We liked each other right away. We formed a band together at Tony's request. Now at the Bohème, the band would play half popular stuff (Michel's passion) and half soul (the up-and-coming music that fascinated me). On Sunday afternoons, the French returnees from Africa held dances and Jewish parties. The place was crowded. Young people came in droves to the soul concerts. Michel and I created a kind of permanent excitement. He was at ease with everything—jazz and popular music, small and large bands, groups that backed big stars. As for me, I introduced my own arrangements and compositions.

"Wana di Lambo"

Singing in African style at this time was mission impossible. The Africans I hired obstinately refused to do so. They wanted to look like Americans and to sing only in English. Bullheaded, I slipped into our repertoire one of my first songs, "Wana di Lambo," sung in Douala. It was one of the songs we would record for Phonogram's export division.

Fine times at the Bohème didn't fill my pockets. Thank God the string of dances hadn't come to an end yet, as we made our exhausting way over the roads. While my work was well known in Africa, I had started over in Paris with nothing, just connections. Dances would begin at about ten. By the time midnight rolled around, I was asleep at my organ. My apprenticeship was a hard one, until the day I discovered Otis Redding and the group Booker T and the MGs—a revelation, a revolution. The quartet brought new color to soul music. Before, an organ player had to stick to jazz and bebop, like Jimmy Smith. Otis's foursome introduced music in double time, which opened up a field of possibilities for me since I was used to the triple time of jazz. Their quartet was clearly going to be a major influence. Donald "Duck" Dunn played bass, Al Jackson drums, and Booker T the amazing organ. I went nuts about this instrument. Tony, very tight with the Americans, had all their American releases imported to the Bohème.

Suddenly my buddy Michel Boss learned that Dick Rivers, one of the idols of the age, was looking to set up a band. Would I finally be able to give up the dance-hall circuit every weekend? I could hardly believe it. Playing with a star like Dick meant becoming one of the elite. Shows lasted only forty-five minutes, but the fee was triple what we got for a dance that lasted all night long. In Paris, the French wanted only their idols: Eddy Mitchell and the Chaussettes Noires, and Dick, the wonderful Dick, whose Lionceaux were climbing the charts to the heavens.

"Try a Little Tenderness"

Coco and I moved to the Faubourg Saint-Martin area of Paris. A clever diplomat, she had managed to persuade the landlord to rent us a big studio apartment, despite the fact that I was black. We had no phone. Martine, who ran the café downstairs, took pity on us and let us make phone calls from her place. Her husband Gerard claimed to be the *bougnat*, the café owner, who cut the thinnest slice of smoked ham in all of Paris. He was a big fan of the Agriculture Expo at the Porte de Versailles. He would go to admire the most modern machinery made for delicatessens, but he remained firmly persuaded that his own abilities were superior to those of the fascinating gadgets.

Dick Rivers had a rehearsal hall loaned to him by Pathé out in Sèvres. We played without stopping from one to five in the morning for a whole month. Dick left us to rehearse in peace. He was happy just to know that his bandleader had things in hand. He was a god in my eyes. For the first time, I was close to a rock 'n' roll star. My entry into the Lionceaux could open doors to radio and television for me, since stars sometimes played live on Raymond Marcillac's and Guy Lux's shows. But the god became all too mortal—we played only five concerts, since Dick had had pretty hazy plans for this tour (which we didn't know, of course). Two concerts in Oran, one in Alger, one on TV and one on radio in Paris.

The Lionceaux had to open a concert in a distant suburb for Nino Ferrer, whose star was also shooting skyward. His hits "Le Téléphone" and "Mirza" were as popular in the chicest neighborhoods as in the most forgotten backwaters. The scheduled concert took place one Sunday afternoon. Before the curtain rose, Nino came to greet us. He spoke to me. His organist wanted to leave him to start his own studio. The organist was a giant, and he looked like a Mr. Wizard gone mad for technology. His trade name was Baron Estardy. Nino sang and accompanied himself on bass. His drummer, Benett, was excellent. Nino asked me to take the place vacated by Baron Estardy. I carefully avoided telling him that the organ and I were not yet friends. I had only practiced on a poor man's instrument, a nothing whose performance capacity was far from rivaling the Hammond—the Rolls-Royce in its category—that Nino possessed for his trio. This Hammond was a monster; I had neither the means to buy one for myself nor the opportunity to play one elsewhere. Without trembling and giving myself away, I agreed to Nino's proposal with a firm and definite yes. I gave him Madame Martine's telephone number. Christmas 1965 arrived, and with it the beginning of a long waiting period down at my bougnat friends. Would Nino follow through?

Michel and I continued our work at the Bohème. We also played the Bilboquet, the Saint-Germain-des-Prés club where rhythm and blues were king. On my own, I continued composing and recording records for Africa. I made the acquaintance of Gérard Davoust, Philips's export division director, who would become an influential international editor later on. He called on me when he needed me, which allowed me to gather my devoted musicians together under my own name. I hired Célia, a woman from Martinique with a strange personality and a voice of gold—the first woman from the islands to have a hit with a Toots Thielemans song, "Jazzy Blue-sette." I also recruited Alan Shelley from Guadeloupe, whose timbre could have been mistaken for that of James Brown. He was a great dancer without a word of English but with the accent and the passion. We played Otis Redding's songs—"Try a Little Tenderness." Our sound was very different from what was on the air: old stuff like the songs of Georges Jouvin et sa Trompette d'Or.

After three weeks I had almost forgotten Nino's proposal. Then the phone call came. Madame Martine's son climbed the stairs four at a time, all excited: "Monsieur Manu, it's Nino Ferrer!" The famous star calling that little bistro—I was bursting with pride. For Nino to reach me there was good for my reputation in the neighborhood. Our neighbors treated us like their mascot. This was how it was for us everywhere we lived in France.

Nino left a message asking me to call him back. Was it real? I called Nino Ferrer from Madame Martine's. His father had a superb apartment in the fancy part of Paris, known as Passy. Nino asked if I was free. I should think so! He set a date with me at his house. He dashed off his repertoire to me because we had to go to Belgium three days later for five scheduled shows and then come back to Paris to play on radio and TV. Nino advised me to go see Baron Estardy, who could explain how to work the organ stops to get the best timbre, sound, and color—specific fingering for a most specific concert tour. I had only three days to swallow it all and master the monster, no wrong notes allowed. Nino's excellent musicians were awaiting me. They were true to the name of their group, Les Requins—real sharks, pros who could play any kind of music and read any sheet music. They commanded high prices for a song, going from studio to studio. They were good jazzmen. I started to develop a complex about this: I was a saxophonist, not an organist. I wasn't sure where the bluff would end. I had to conquer the beast in three days. I sketched the positions of the stops and wrote down their numbers, measure after measure.

Nino had wanted a black guy.

I'd Like to Be
a Black Man

APPEARANCES WERE PRESERVED: I was an African, with ebony skin and my laugh was louder than the one on the Banania commercial, which came in handy. Nino fantasized about Uncle Tom, the cotton fields, and the Mississippi. My images were real, of African palm and coconut trees. "Je voudrais être un noir" ["I'd like to be a black man"], Nino Ferrer sang. His voice was superb; he loved jazz. My presence added a little extra color. Everything was smiling on him. Eddie Barclay had just opened an unlimited line of credit for him. After three days of hasty rehearsal we left for Belgium, where the first concert was to take place. Fear paralyzed me. I was sweating from every pore. If I didn't work out, it would all be over for me. Sentiment had no place in this business; reason was king. That didn't shock me: I wanted to have a head that cool. In the future, out of emotional weakness, I would keep musicians who hurt me professionally because I didn't dare kick them out.

The Belgian tour turned into just one concert. Immediately we returned to Paris, where France-Inter radio had programmed a show with the band. Would I be asked to participate? The first evening had been a test. Nino didn't say anything about it. The Requins, who accompanied him on stage and years later would form Jacques Martin's band, were completely silent. Was I any good or not? No one could be bothered to answer. My colleagues didn't know how I had met Nino and whether he was attached to me; their fee was too juicy to take the least risk. Doudou, the Caribbean bassist, took a complicit stance. My waiting became feverish. Still Nino said nothing. My engagement with him was far from certain. An endless week went by; then a phone call at Madame Martine's: we were to go on tour to Dijon and the surrounding area. Michel Fugain, who was just starting his career, would join us. Eddy Mitchell was the lead act, with his hit, "Il y a Toujours un Petit Coin Qui Me Rappelle" ["There's Always a Little Spot That Reminds Me"]. In my eyes, he was the typical French rocker. My favorite remained Dick Rivers—less sexy perhaps, but so much closer to Presley's spirit. Dick always avoided looking as though he took his work too seriously, when in fact he worked like a dog. And above all, he was funny.

I accompanied Fugain, who was also jumping into the lions' den for the first time. We both had the jitters. I kept one foot in show biz and the other in the dance-hall world. Whew! Nino had gigs all the time. In between, a little country dance was always nice. Our tour, organized by one of the Marouani sons, came off successfully. Nino put an American car at the band's disposal; he himself drove a splendid Jag. Sometimes he wanted me with him. Traveling around with a star in a Jaguar made the fans look at and like me more. In radio and TV studios, Nino demanded my presence.

Such adventures! On the road to Brussels we burned out the motor—not for failing to warn the driver. The red dashboard light had been coming on for a while. "Careful!" yelled one of the musicians, a guy from Aix-en-Provence with that typical Midi accent. Pierre Houassian, who was of Armenian descent and often accompanied Charles Aznavour, had warned the driver in vain. The car refused to start, smoke seeping from the hood. It was six o'clock in the morning. The wake-up was brutal. "We warned you. You're nuts. Go get some help at the farm you see over there," we demanded of the driver. The man, Francis Cournet, was a real shark. He had two notebooks in his pockets: a red one in which he wrote the names of his debtors and a black one in which he kept the list of all his business he didn't want to declare. He was very talented but didn't give a shit about the work; he just wanted the money. He went to the farm and was attacked by a dog, who destroyed his pants. He came back to the car white with fury, the dog hanging off him. "I bought these jeans yesterday—they cost me my right arm!" We were crazy with worry because Nino was waiting for us. How to get started again? Finally a mechanic agreed to tow us. We were not late for the concert. Our various adventures sometimes felt like miracles.

"La Vie Parisienne"

The ORTF [the French radio and television bureau] was courting Nino Ferrer. We rambled through its halls. "Manu, over here; Manu, over there." Nino introduced me to everyone. My brain was starting to go "tilt" because I had no competition; I was practically the only black man around. At that time, show business counted just one Caribbean, Henri Salvador, and one mixed-race Frenchman, spirituals singer John William. From January to June 1967, it was one party after another; frenetic. I bought a car—a sturdy VW 1200.

At the beginning of July, we emigrated to the Côte d'Azur. The Marouanis arranged it so distances between different concerts weren't so great. They rented a villa near Saint-Tropez for all of us. We rehearsed assiduously. The public loved Nino. He thought of everything. He had convinced the owner of the Maxi Voum Voum, a club in Juan-les-Pins, to let us play there when we were not in concert. In Antibes, the annual jazz festival was moving into high gear. Miles Davis was its star. He brought his amorous conquests over to dance at the Maxi Voum Voum. "God has descended among us . . ." Anxiety seized us. In fact, Miles couldn't have cared less; he had just come there to cruise. I played my tenor sax fervently. The year 1967 ended in euphoria. In Paris between tours, I played sax regularly at the Bilboquet and with my own band, created for my African-export recordings. It included the inimitable Célia; singer Alan Shelley; bassist Jeannot Dikoto, also known as Karl, my Cameroonian friend; a second saxophonist, Mam Houari, a mixed-race man of Arab descent; and Vincent, a Tunisian-born Frenchman.

One partying night, Nino Ferrer showed up at the Bilboquet with Eddy Mitchell. He came down to the floor where we were playing. Incredible! "What? Manu, you play sax? You never told me!" I retorted, "You never asked me." Nino didn't miss a beat: "Starting next week, you're my bandleader. With your sax." I had been promoted. The old leader was fired. With my new power, I hired Jeannot the bassist. Our group imitated Otis Redding's band and played his songs. Tour dates multiplied beyond the borders of France. Nino was afraid of planes, so we dragged around in a bus to the farthest ports of the Adriatic.

The period was a luxurious one. Coco followed me everywhere in this "vie parisienne," as light as Jacques Offenbach's music. I accompanied Nino; I went to the Bilboquet; I entered the Club de l'Etoile, a snooty spot on Avenue Victor Hugo, forbidden to all blacks except musicians. Charlie, the owner, had invited for a season some Americans who played a kind of soul music. Madame de Rothschild paid for my services at an intimate gathering of four hundred. I recruited Africans for my own band, which was no mean responsibility: during a party at the Tour d'Argent, some of them got so drunk the waiters had to drag them out like corpses. I lost money on my brothers. We moved forward like crabs, catching good deals and then forgetting ourselves. My compatriots repaid me unkindly, and I was the one who ended up catching hell. When the time came to collect fees, I took twenty francs more than the others. What a scandal! They demanded equality. It was atavistic—value counted for nothing; it wasn't respected. In the same way, back home, everything was done by decree. But that's another story.

"Salt Pop Corn"

My career as a bandleader took on new dimensions. At Phonogram-Philips I was in charge of the Africa division. I wrote a brilliant, screaming instrumental piece, "Salt Pop Corn," which mixed rhythm and blues, a little funk, and a pop sound behind it. It lacked the truly African character that would be found in my later music. Of course, the record was destined only for Africa. How to take a small step toward musical openness in France? One of my friends had a specialty shop in a Champs-Elysées arcade. I gave him a copy of "Salt Pop Corn." The store always displayed best-selling records. In two weeks, my song was ahead of James Brown's—unbelievable but true. I dashed over to Philips with the good news. My welcome was an embarrassed one: the unforseeable success of my recording was awkward because the record had been made for export. The company's directors took a month to concoct a plan. They agreed to bring out my record in France, but with another jacket and no promotion. My struggle had in any case given me a tiny push forward, "Manu's music can work here; maybe we should put his records out in France . . ."

But alas, we were not at that point yet.

Big Band

Into this cultural melting pot jumped Légitimus. An exuberant Caribbean, he was a real force of nature. His mother was an actress, and one of his relations was a well-known politician in Guadeloupe. The family headed a famous band in Paris. The guy called me over one night while I was playing at the Bohème. "I really like what you're doing. I have an offer to make you, poorly paid—150 francs [about thirty dollars]." Légitimus, who had to produce a fifteen-minute television show, wanted to pull together a high-caliber group. Could I help him? "Yes, of course," I answered, with my usual bravado. I was interested in the chance to appear on television heading a band, rare on TV. Légitimus had already talked to a few Caribbeans, who had refused because of the tiny fee. He became stubborn and with my help managed to pull together a band. His quarter-hour on the air was such a triumph that the show immediately became a monthly one, entitled "Pulsations." It went on for two and a half years, first in black and white and then in color. Big-name singer Claude Nougaro agreed to sponsor the whole thing and even wrote a song in its honor. For us, it was an opportunity to be seized, a stage that would take us beyond our narrow existence of dance-hall musicians. Légitimus asked me to arrange one of his pieces to serve as our theme song. The bells sounded, and with them—fame. "Pulsations" made history. It was the first show on which Caribbeans, Africans, and French people formed a heterogeneous group, able to accompany any artist on television. I brought in my friend Slim Pezin and others. Our big band pulled together, just as in a love story.

I dreamed of Count Basie's and Duke Ellington's bands. Those masters had had a love affair lasting forty years with their musicians, who never left them. During this long marriage, hatred and passions flowed, but their union was never destroyed. They belonged to something like the same religion, something they believed in from the start. This faith is the most beautiful thing in the world because no contract can create it. From such a fountain spring great men. With my first band formed for television, I started to dream big.

Christmas 1967 approached. Mike Brant, with his beautiful voice, tried his luck in France. He came to the Club de l'Etoile. We sat in and became friends. Jean Renard, that celebrated hit-maker, melted listening to Mike's voice and cooked him up a hit, "Laisse-Moi T'Aimer" ["Let Me Love You"]. I was the first one to rehearse the number with him. Recording started. On Christmas Eve, Mike Brant had his first "tour date" at a very hip club in Meudon-la Forêt. Instantly he ascended to idol-heaven. Like the comic book heroes of *Pieds-Nickelés*, we rose to the challenge of the TV screen. On some wild shows, he would do Jerry Lewis and I Ray Charles.

In this milieu, people were surprised to see an African with such pretensions—a nut in action. Coco fervently supported me; she played the manager very effectively. Professionals accepted me, and the public saw me on television more and more often. In the neighborhood and at Madame Martine's, people were more than a little proud: "Manu's leading a band!" Everything was working, I had found a niche, and—what's more—I had no competitors. But I was still not making records. I was part of that hip set of people who were as much technicians as musicians. There was a handful of us operating in Paris, Africans and French people who liked American sounds and yet could appreciate the Beatles. Our feet were firmly anchored on the ground. So much the better!

The only mainstream music magazine at the time was *Salut les Copains*, which was aimed at the young fans of mainstream artists such as Sylvie Vartan. *SLC*'s pages were closed to the "lower" types of music. Soul couldn't get in; pop, its flowers, and Nepal distantly stuck up their noses. In the United States, Jimi Hendrix played the first megaconcert of the century, with five hundred thousand in the audience. The wave was rising; we could feel it swelling. We chose soul rather than rock. Hendrix connected the two. He was at the forefront, reconciling styles and people with his guitar. Rock's martial rhythm was not natural to me. As opposed to jazz and soul, which were soft, rock music was for rowdies. We heard tales about the way some American concerts ended, guitars in pieces and organs overturned. Far from this sound and fury, the soft generation got stoned on Nepal. The growing conflict was magnified by the events of May 1968.

May 1968

History decided to upset everyone's routine. May 1968 turned France upside-down. Hundreds of thousands of students and workers marched on the capital and in the large provincial cities. A nearly general strike paralyzed the country. President de Gaulle no longer knew where to hide. Quietly, he went to Baden-Baden to consult with his generals. We carefree guys knew nothing about this revolution, these "real things," as we called them back home. Far from the paving-stone projectiles of Saint-Germain, we were touring with Nino Ferrer on the beaches of southern Italy. Our concerts over, we had to return to France, and so we took the Swiss railroads. Since no trains were running in France, we were stuck. I had no visa to stay in the country; I only had one for Italy. I couldn't go forward and I couldn't go back. We were stalled with our instruments and our bags, forbidden to set foot outside the Geneva train station. My colleagues spent the day in unbelievable negotiations, looking for a transport company that could ensure our return to Paris. It was no simple thing to come to an agreement during these uncertain weeks in the happy month of May. Finally, the owner of a Mercedes bus agreed to take the whole group. Our tons of equipment were put in storage. The driver, as a respectful Swiss, did not permit himself to drive faster than sixty kilometers an hour between Geneva and Paris. After this exhausting crossing, we found Paris dead.

May of 1968 broke our stride. Damn! The summer tour we had planned fell apart, most of the fifty parties having been canceled. Our savings melted away. It would take us months—until the beginning of 1970—to heal.

The machinery reluctantly got back into gear. Our shows with Légitimus picked up again, and we still did some concerts with Nino. He was going through a period of doubt and anxiety. His shining star darkened. Moreover, he had little respect for his own hits—"Le Téléphone," "Mirza,"—that had given him his reputation. Perhaps he would have liked to write like Brassens or Brel. He was disenchanted, frustrated by the feeling of having gotten off track. We were just a painter's palette that he hardly appreciated anymore; we teetered precariously behind him. He rejected his own talent, which he deemed minor. He was chewing himself up inside, yet he was full of talent. What a mistake! I loved the world he managed to create in his songs. "La Maison Près de la Fontaine" ["The House near the Fountain"] and "Le Sud" ["The South"] were almost like paintings. Living with the guy who composed and played these songs was very good for me. My collaboration with him was one of the most positive in my whole life.

But we didn't inhabit the same South. His was the South of Louisiana and Italy; mine remained that of Africa, under the Abidjan and Douala skies. Twenty years later, this uncomfortable fit would savagely reappear. In July 1988, the Francofolies at La Rochelle dedicated an evening to me, La Fête à Manu, my first event as an

African. I was free to bring on my musical brothers, the Cameroonian band Les Têtes Brûlées, Maxime Le Forestier, . . . and Nino. It
was an honor, a gesture of pride, and a responsibility my adoptive
country offered me. I arranged "Le Sud" in my own way, according
to my own sounds and colors. I used the kora in it. Nino had a hard
time singing to it and had to get used to it. While he understood
why I was doing it my way, he couldn't handle it. Ten minutes before
he was to go on, he broke down. Nino will always have my respect.
The rest—well, that's life!

But at the beginning of 1969, Nino grew progressively apart
from our group. We ended up separating quietly, with much left
unsaid. Thank God, Gérard Davoust from Philips was watching over
me. He introduced me to the music producer of the Tutti company.

Saxy Party

I finally signed my first recording contract. Its financial conditions
were draconian. Happily, however, Tutti records got lots of airplay.
My mixed-style music filled the need for a rhythmic instrumental
music of a color different from that of the American bands or the
big bands like Raymond Lefebvre's. I began to be heard regularly
on radio. I took in substantial royalties. But we still had to talk serious money; the worth of the music was not enough. As an African
from a member country of the CFA zone, my fee would be spent
in francs—that many more dollars saved that wouldn't fly off to the
United States.

Gérard Davoust had a good nose without adequate means to
achieve his ambitions. He kept wanting to help me. Sometimes he
would bring me *kwela* records from South Africa. Sometimes he had
me listen to reggae, which was new to me. "These things, you know,
one day . . . ," he would insist, to get me to try new genres. Gérard
Davoust's plans finally came to fruition. In fall of 1969, I recorded
my first album under the name Manu with Philips, who handled its
distribution in France. *Saxy Party* included the illustrious favorites
of the day, such as Georges Moustaki's "Le Métèque" ["The Foreigner," pejoratively]. I was also able to introduce my own songs,
such as "Tele Miso" ["Open Your Eyes" in Douala], in which for
the first time I used a chorus.

I'm no singer; I'm a musician. But Louis Armstrong haunted me
as a model. He played trumpet like a god and used his voice to give
his music a human touch the cold metal instrument couldn't give. I

had all his records. Before I ever understood English, Armstrong's voice and trumpet had blown me away. So why not try to follow his example? Even if the public couldn't understand my Douala, voices could be a connection to instruments. I also decided to enrich the whole thing by adding choruses in the background. How to recruit choruses, since I couldn't sing in French? In studios, professional chorus members were all Europeans. This posed an additional challenge—finding words in Douala that made sense, sounded right, *and* could be pronounced by Europeans.

My producer was a black American who had American prestige and sounds. The engineers were perplexed when faced with music they didn't know. Our sound had not yet crossed the Atlantic, as far as they knew. They were used to accordion tunes, classical, and Latin music. What a place! In recording, the technicians became fearful when they heard the volume of our bass—"The needle's going into the red!" To us, the bass was the belly, the core of the music. "Your technique is nowhere," they told us. And we answered them, "OK, but your ears are nowhere." We advised them to listen to James Brown's records, with his bass and drums. The technicians ended up getting excited about what we were bringing them. As for the Africans, they didn't miss a chance; I frequently lost face. Jeannot, a good-looking man and a skirt-chaser, was hard to catch. He would sleep wherever and whenever sleep overtook him. Sometimes he arrived in the studio hours late. But he brought a sound of unequaled color. The mood withstood all of these trials and remained good-natured.

Benefiting from the latest in technology, the album *Saxy Party* finally came out. The first criticism: "It's jazzy. Too bad your name isn't more American—you'd become better-known. Dibango sounds too traditional." Too bad I was neither Latin American nor black American; African creativity was hard for French people to sell. I wouldn't abandon my family name at any price. Dibango I am, Dibango I will remain.

"Idiba"

SAXY PARTY CHECKMATED SUCCESS. My instrumental album met with critical acclaim yet sold poorly. No hits emerged, but radio stations liked it as background music. My pockets grew holes; I was at bottom again, back in my threadbare saddle. My collaboration with Nino had dead-ended. Once again I was playing dance halls and those endless nights in the country. I started going around again to the Paris nightclubs in Saint-Germain-des-Près and Montparnasse.

The Maxi Voum Voum in Juan-les-Pins wanted me to form a band for the summer. On July 19, that famous day when the first American astronaut set foot on the moon, we were playing in the Maxi Voum Voum's electric penumbra. We worked what was once our smash repertoire into the ground. The crowds turned up their noses. In a few months, things had changed significantly. For the first time in my career, I didn't know which way the wind was blowing. We kept playing rhythm and blues, but the audiences wanted rock or pop, "peace and love," California-style stuff. I was ashamed; I was no longer giving the public what it wanted. The owner kicked us out before the season ended. Though he had broken the contract, I didn't dare ask for anything. We clearly hadn't cut it. We came home to Paris with our tails between our legs and our pockets empty.

Returning to the capital, I hooked up with a Jewish woman who owned the Chevaliers du Temple club, a basement-level hot spot in the Marais district. Sarah made frequent trips to the United States to bring back a harvest of records. She had lots of friends she had met on the American bases around Paris during the Liberation. Her customers would abandon the Left Bank and flock to the Chevaliers du Temple around midnight. She kept everyone up until five in the morning. All the musicians of the time came by. I started a band at Sarah's. The work was steady, but poorly paid.

I was searching for myself.

"Ngolowake"

Rather than sticking to rhythm and blues and pop, I took a trip back to my African roots. I held onto both of my hats: one repertoire for Paris, another one for Africa. The spirit of open-mindedness represented by *Saxy Party* was gone. Opportunity was closing up again, even for black American artists, whose eclipse lasted a few more years. Jazz and rhythm and blues were to suffer because of this. It would take the arrival of madmen like Patrice Blanc-Franquart and Jean-Claude Lattès's brother to smash the barriers and permit musicians to rise. Our rejection started in 1969. We bathed in Californian sounds with the ease of fish out of water. The Chevaliers du Temple was a rare harbor where we could breathe.

Still and always from New York came soul music. Blacks affirmed their race, sought their roots. As an African, I knew who I was and where I was born. While Léopold Senghor was publishing his poems, the first black films were being made in the United States. I liked this new trend; it helped me affirm myself. I became passionate about Black Power. I was overwhelmed by the immense civil rights demonstrations organized by Dr. Martin Luther King, during which numerous men and women paid with their lives to improve conditions for blacks. Novelist Chester Himes and his picturesque heroes Grave Digger Jones and Coffin Ed Johnson, supercops, guided us around Harlem. The New World was sending word, but the banks of the Hudson were still far away. I dreamed of visiting the land of my idols, of seeing my favorite musicians play; of course they would be fantastic. I had an inferiority complex about it. Who was I compared to these American superblacks, creators of music and brilliant technicians?

I didn't know yet what I was searching for, but I was sure I had something on my African side. Parisian producers were interested in me. On the other hand, the financial arrangements Philips could promise me were mediocre. That company kept me stuck playing for anyone and everyone. I had to bring out my *Saxy Party* on Tutti.

Joseph Kabasélé came through Paris with Don Gonzalo, my Cuban friend, king of the *charanga*. He invited me to accompany them on four records made for Africa at Decca. Together we started out under the name African Team. Good show.

Kabasele had worked with this company a long time; Rolande Lecouviour was head of its Africa Division. Decca's catalog was the richest of any: the Rolling Stones, Julio Iglesias, Raymond Legrand and his big band. Raymond, who was Michel's father and Colette Renard's husband, had taken a shine to me when I was playing in clubs in Brittany during the summer of 1966.

Rolande Lecouviour discovered me. My arrangements struck her just right. African Team was doing well in Africa. Rolande became my accomplice; her friendship continued until the day she died. She wanted me to come over to Decca. How could I break my contract with Philips? Gérard Davoust helped me get out cleanly. Decca produced my second record. It had no title, but the songs were immediate hits with the African public. I was in a state of grace. . .

"Soma Loba"

The record opened the gates to Cameroon and the 1970s for me. The music forced people to dance. I sang about everyday events. "Soma Loba" means "Thank God" in Douala. On this album without a name, Francis Bébey—married to one of my cousins, and having just procured a contract with Philips thanks to me—composed "Idiba" ["Morning"], whose symbolism was clear. You mustn't lower your head, nor deny yourself; you must walk straight ahead. . . . This challenge upset the country a bit. I did two arrangements of it: one for him, with very sober orchestration; the other for me, with an eye to making my album. Francis sang, accompanying himself on the guitar, with a bassist, my vibraphone, and light percussion.

My version enjoyed enormous success in Cameroon and the rest of the continent, the only real love story I had with my country. "Ngolowake," my favorite song, made families talk among themselves. I composed it and wrote the words. It dealt humorously with an eternal theme: the greed of men and women from our country. The former, looking for women, never have enough money; the latter always want more for a purpose that remains secret. My version of "Idiba" provoked lively debate in Cameroon. Young people adored me. The press was unreservedly in my favor. With "Idiba," people discovered that within the same language and the same framework, a song can be totally transformed by a different artist. My version became their favorite. The public enjoyed thinking I was in competition with other artists who were used to this game. I hadn't sung the song, they said, I had "stolen" it.

Because of these songs, Cameroonians understood that music could go beyond its usual limits. Playing with double entendres fascinated me. In the months that followed, I wrote (in French) "Pour une Poignée de CFA" ["For a Handful of CFA Francs"], in which I affirmed that for a fistful of money some would sell father and mother—a clever way to talk about the neighborhood business and goings-on. I messed with the way the public understood the song, and people didn't realize it until later. I went even further: "Afrique sans Fric" ["No-Cash Africa"] was a song about the two Africas, "*Afrique à fric*" [the one "with cash"] and "*Afrique sans fric*" [the one without]. I would later open concerts during meetings of heads of state with this song. Fifteen years later, Ivoirian singer Alpha Blondy would make these humorous kinds of declarations in his own reggae style.

When it came out in 1969, the album without a name brought me many invitations. I made frequent round-trips, for example, to the church in Douala, where the pastor liked my music; to the OAU; and to the large international organizations which called me to play in Kinshasa, Dakar, or Abidjan.

I traveled alone. These countries still didn't have the means to invite a whole band, so I created one on-site each time. I had two weeks' rehearsal before the concert. Oh my God! I hardly had time to play tourist. The local musicians would welcome me warmly. They did their best, and I tried to share my love of music with them. They didn't have the cynicism of the Requins in Paris. They didn't have sophisticated studios, and they didn't even know how to read music, but this didn't stop them—all I had to do was give them a little time in order to obtain surprising results. They really gave of themselves, like those jazzmen who knew nothing about sight-reading or like Django Reinhardt, a guitar genius despite his burned fingers. This was how I organized the first workshops—musical ones—on African soil. The experience was a little frustrating but richly promising. History took giant steps. When the independence celebrations began, traditional groups had played the official parties. Since that time, the kids had grown up, and they wanted to learn music. Côte d'Ivoire and Niger asked me to start a band in a month or two. Everywhere I worked with local musicians. Our exchange was of a rare quality. When they became famous, they kept their workshop spirit. I left an impression on them, as they did on me.

Every country receives the same kinds of music and adapts them; each person hears meter in his or her own way. My trip extended from Togo to Benin via Lagos—and with what stopovers! Cameroon wanted a national orchestra. Three of us were named by the government to audition candidates. They came from north and south; even traditional musicians came. The authorities did not ask for our opinion. Their only concern was a certain balance between the different ethnic groups: each was to be represented within this embryo of a band. This became a melodrama in which music took a back seat. We had no say about the subject of the audition material; a famous man overseeing things had selected "Laura," an American tune even the most illustrious jazz musicians had a hard time playing. How to play "Laura" on tam-tams or balafon? In the audition hall, the candidates started by listening to a version of "Laura" on the record player. At the first chord, their faces would twist. They really had to perform now. Some didn't even try. "Sir, I don't know that piece. I can't play." They wished they had stayed in their villages. How could we grade them under these conditions? We gave our evaluations, but the authorities took over our grading system and designated their own candidates. Using our presence on the jury, they bragged on radio about having set up a professional selection process. What was it—willful vice, incompetence, or lack of awareness? Twenty years later, Cameroon is overflowing with musical potential but still doesn't have a national orchestra worthy of the name.

Ryco Jazz

In this beginning of the 1970s, traveling around freelance, I rediscovered my own country. The monk I had been was defrocked in this life of easy pleasures. Sensual Douala, Yaoundé the powerful capital—I became inebriated by them. I succumbed to the charms of Cameroon; its sweet invitations seduced me.

Drunk on this flattering fluttering about me, I took advantage to connect with French people who liked African music and the African way of life. They tended to work for emerging commercial companies such as Air Afrique. On stops in Paris, they would come to the Chevaliers du Temple to feel at home again. When they returned to the [African] continent, they invited me to play private parties—the Lions Club, the Rotary. They believed in my talent. I worked frenetically, organizing numerous workshops. My nameless album continued to sell. I recorded more 45s with Decca.

Soon I had only one idea: to play in Cameroon, to take some action in my own country. At this blessed moment I met Jerry Malekani Bokilo, the Zairean guitarist. He led Ryco Jazz, a band whose reputation was incredible. He had lived for the past five years in the Antilles, where he had introduced the African idea of clustering guitars previously unknown there. Ryco Jazz was the first African band to become a favorite in Guadeloupe and Martinique. Their triumph had aroused jealousy; Jerry and his band had finally had to leave. Jerry and I immediately became inseparable. I adored his talent as an instrumentalist; he loved my songs. We played together all the time. It was heavenly. Quite naturally, I brought him into what I was doing.

The eighth Tropics Soccer Cup, the African cup, was to take place in Yaoundé in 1972. All Cameroon was getting ready. I went there for a concert and got the notion of trying to hit it big again, as I had in 1964 when I had written "Flottez Drapeaux sur Yaoundé," based on a hymn, for the first cup. The eighth was shaping up like a world's fair—a challenge. I asked for an audience with the minister of sports to see if he would release funds for me to record an original composition. The government would pay for the pressing and distribute it free to all participants. It was not an easy battle, since I was not the only one with the idea. But my nameless album instilled general confidence. The minister gave me a million CFA francs [twenty thousand French francs, or four thousand dollars] to produce my 45. I ran to Douala to tell my father the good news. At our family home, I took out my million in bills, folded inside a newspaper. A long silence. My father looked at it. He had never seen so much money. He called my mother. She ran out of the kitchen, speechless. My father said, "There are things happening in this country. The president has given your son a million francs to go make noise."

I threw myself into the work body and soul. On one side of the 45 I recorded the hymn; on the other I recorded "Soul Makossa," written using a traditional makossa rhythm with a little soul thrown in. In my Douala neighborhood, at my parents' house, I rehearsed this second piece. The house had no air-conditioning, and the windows were wide open. All the kids flocked around. Hearing me rehearse, they fell over laughing. Unbelievable—how on earth had I concocted *that* mishmash? Poor makossa really took a blow. My father was astonished: "Can't you pronounce 'makossa' like everyone else? You stutter: 'mamako mamasa.' You think they're going to accept that in Yaoundé?" The Cup organizing committee reacted the same way. The march on side one they found "impeccable." But the other side . . . "Really, Manu has gone nuts. What possesses him to stutter like that?" I hardly cared. The million CFA francs I had received in Yaoundé were enough to satisfy my ambition. I was a million miles away from picturing the staggering fate destined for "Soul Makossa." Distributed as a gift, my memorable 45 was a flop. Cameroon lost the eighth cup to the Congo, 8 to 1. Furious fans broke my delightful disk in pieces. Sad end for a hymn. . .

I returned to Paris. Jerry hadn't left me. We decided to fly to Algeria because Sonatour, the official Algerian tourist agency, was recruiting bands to play at its resorts. Our quickly concluded engagement was for one month. Jerry was the backbone of the band with his guitar. We hired a French bassist; a Congolese singer, Freddy Nkounkou; and a Guadeloupean drummer, Jobi Dandelery, and tumba player, Mano Rodanet. We didn't even have a repertoire. We rehearsed two songs slightly, one of which was "Soul Makossa." Destination: Zéralda, a vacation town brilliantly designed by the architect Fernand Pouillon. A breath of freedom floated us there. . .

"Nights in Zéralda"

Each of us had brought his roots with him to Zéralda. We had no cares other than performing three hours every evening for the vacationers, who were mostly foreigners. The vacation club's managers left us alone, only too happy about our fruitful relaxation. The evening's "stage" was the Raïma, an arena-shaped site in a valley. On the heights gathered Algerians from the surrounding areas who couldn't afford to come to the club. Enthusiasm would crest as soon as we started the chant to "Soul Makossa." Word of mouth spread, and people made a real effort to come. We surpassed ourselves. A solo from Jerry or an unusual flight on sax brought back the enthusiasm every time. It was as though we were playing chess with the audience. Going on stage, we would start to joke among ourselves, just to create the right ambiance. The audience caught our tension and ran with it. Our keepers were satisfied and extended our contract to four months.

Our days were free, our lodgings elegant and spacious. We rehearsed and conversed euphorically. We improvised enormously, to fill in the meager repertoire we had brought from Paris. Over the course of our improvisations a certain spirit was born among us, an extraordinary field of exploration. With help from the equipment, and not an instant's laziness, we composed what would ultimately become my basic stock in trade. Our unconstrained life-style no doubt inspired me more than any affinity with Muslim Algeria. The modest fee we received was not needed for the local stores, and we regularly transferred our savings to Paris.

The essential thing remained the music. In our bags we had what we needed to nourish us—albums by Miles Davis and by a band of dissidents who had just left him. Miles brought me to the soprano sax. I was in love with his muted trumpet and the new sound space it offered. This space totally worked with the spirit moving us. Feverishly, I resumed playing soprano sax, the instrument I had barely touched since the early sixties in Belgium. Sometimes Miles Davis had a genius for opening up new horizons to all musicians. Our searching took his current and enriched it with our roots.

Depending on the clientele at our performances, an idea might develop that we would start working with. Using my Sony, we recorded every evening's performance. The same went for our daily rehearsals. At night, back in the fold, we would listen to the tapes. New ideas melded, which we tested immediately the next night. "Nights in Zéralda" was one of these pieces, composed live. The echo of these songs would be remembered in Algeria and in the United States, where they would become hits.

Since we liked what we were doing, we were strong. But our happiness came to an end. From Zéralda, we went to Tipaza and Moretti for some vacation concerts before returning to Paris for good. Rather broke that autumn of 1972, I ran to Decca studios to record our Zéralda productions. Miles Davis remained our point of reference. He was the only truly inventive one who dared to have electric piano, acoustic piano, synthesizer, guitar, and trumpet play on the same piece. His palette was surrealistic; thus, on a recent album, he mixed Herbie Hancock, Chick Corea, and Keith Jarrett.

With my Zéralda buddies I recorded a skeleton over which we added several keyboards, following Miles's example—an innovation. *O Boso*, our album, opened up the possibility for fame across the Atlantic. On one side was "Soul Makossa."

Manu's parents (Doula, 1938)

Manu (age four) on the compound

Manu in his departure suit in Douala, ready to leave for France

Manu (age 15) at his first summer camp with his buddies
from Saint Calais in the Sarthe region

Manu the Cub Scout with all the members of his
mother's side of the family

Manu in the student band in Paris with Koka Mpondo, drummer; Michel Doo-Kingué (known as "Chet Davis"), trumpet player; Robert Benn's Ndiné on toumba; "Juanito" Soppo Priso on maracas (Summer 1956)

Manu's professional beginnings at the Tabou; photo taken by Coco (Brussels, 1957)

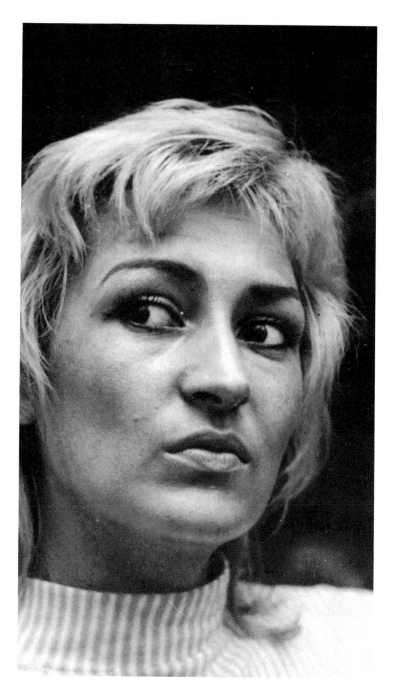

Coco (Brussels, 1957)

Fax Clark at the Tabou (Brussels, 1957)

Manu with Art Blakey, founder of the Jazz Messengers (Brussels, 1959)

Manu's television premiere with Vicky Down's group (Brussels, 1958)

Fonseca and Coco (Brussels, 1958)

The heavyweights of African Jazz (from left to right): Manu,
Tabu-Ley Rochereau, Docteur Nico, the Governor, the driver, Kabasele,
and Roger Izeidi (Stanleyville, 1971)

Manu, Coco, and Franck Iassan at the Afro-Négro (Kinshasa, 1962)

Manu at his first club, the Tam-Tam in Kinshasa (1962)

Manu at the second Tam-Tam, in Douala (1963)

Coco's first visit to Manu's parents' home in Douala (1963)

Manu's beginnings as a bandleader, with Nino Ferrer;
Doudou, bass; Pierre Houassian, tenor sax; Michel Bosal,
trumpet; and Francis Cournet, baritone sax (1967)

Manu with Rolande Lecouviour, his friend who headed the
African pop division at Decca (1972)

Manu with Ahmet Ertegun, who headed Atlantic Records
and offered him a contract at the Apollo in Harlem
(Chevaliers du Temple, Paris, 1973)

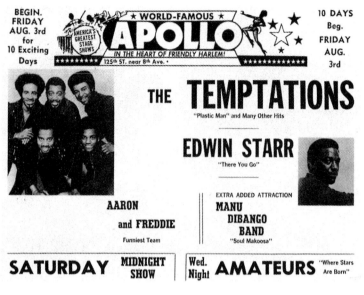

Manu's concert program at the Apollo

Manu in Harlem (1973)

Manu on stage at the Apollo (1973)

Manu and his band at the Apollo in Harlem (1973)

Manu with Bella Bellow (Decca Studios, 1973)

Manu and his African fans

Manu leading Radio-Télévision Ivoirienne's first band with
the Ivoirian singer Aïcha Koné (Abidjan, 1976)

Workshop in Lomé, Togo, with a military band (1976)

First meeting with Hervé Bourges, then the director of the
Ecole de Journalisme (Yaoundé, 1976)

Manu at the Olympia with Bruno Coquatrix (1978)

Manu the bandleader

Manu does ads

Rhoda Scott at Manu's nightclub, Soir au Village (Yaoundé, 1981)

Manu with his daughter Georgia (Paris, 1988)

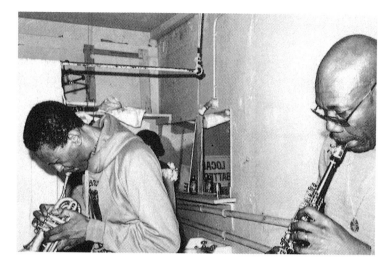

Don Cherry and Manu on tour (Casino de Paris)

Manu with Hervé Bourges during "Tam-Tam pour l'Ethiopie" (1983)

Manu, Johnny Clegg, and Mory Kanté with musicians during
the Printemps de Bourges festival (1988)

Manu with Harry Belafonte during a UNICEF
trip to Zimbabwe (1988)

Manu with Herbie Hancock during production of
Electric Africa (Paris, 1986)

Manu with Miriam Makeba (1987)

Manu with Stevie Wonder (Lagos, Nigeria, 1978)

Manu with Sam Woodyard, Duke Ellington's drummer
for fifteen years (Paris, late 1970)

Manu in Kingston, Jamaica (1979)

The treasury house in Douala in the 1930s; photo by Goethe
(Papa Gotté), who came from Sierra Leone in 1927, bringing
photography and soccer to Cameroon

"Soul Makossa"

WHO WOULD HAVE GUESSED "Soul Makossa" held the slightest makings of a hit? Certainly not us. And Zéralda was no more than a memory.

Strange blacks wandered around Decca's hallways like E.T.s landed from the United States. They looked like those droll, devious preachers born of Chester Himes's imagination. They ran one of the first black production companies started on American soil. Looking for mythical roots from Africa, they were headhunters come to harvest among the capitals of Europe. Who would notice them here? Rolande Lecouviour patiently detailed the virtues of her catalog of records destined for the African market. They weighed what she said, stingy with their comments. For good measure, Rolande, who was ready to sacrifice anything to give me more weight in their eyes, gave them a copy of the 45 I had made for the eighth Tropics Cup in Yaoundé, the only copy that had escaped the massacre.

When they went home, these characters managed to flood the airwaves with "Soul Makossa." Copies sold by the hundreds, thanks to pirating. But we never heard the good news; Paris was deaf to voices from beyond the Atlantic. In the United States, blacks finally saw the record swiped from them by a white recording company with more money. *O Boso* had just come out in France. Americans began swarming to Decca to stock up. "What ridiculous taste they have; they're just grown-up kids . . ." I was their last concern. I didn't cost much: with no promotion, their Zairian productions brought in money. What else could I hope for? As an African, I couldn't aim for the lights of fame, as I was made to understand quite clearly. Their attitude was very uncool.

The world shifted: the petroleum crisis had just erupted. Decca's leaders, comfortably resting on their forty-year reputation, had already lost it without knowing it. They ran the company with ease. They set themselves to distributing the Rolling Stones and the big names of the sixties. In fact, they were firmly mired in the past and blind to the future. What revelation could they see in "Soul Makossa"? "Manu—having a hit? What a joke!" The producer of the group Village People, Henri Belolo, went to New York. He spent an evening in a club whose "star" was [Aristotle] Onassis, who kept asking for "Soul Makossa" so he could dance to it. Onassis thus blessed the song. The French producer couldn't keep from letting Paris know about that, which garnered me some small amount of credibility. Just a bit.

Yet Decca's American orders suddenly rose like yeasted bread in the space of a week and a half: five thousand copies, then thirty thousand. This might have aroused the directors' curiosity, but no: an African from Douala *couldn't* have an international hit. Paternalism was still going strong. It was impossible for them to realize that Mamadou, the child colonized in the whites' schoolbooks, had finally grown up. They had the same reaction toward the newly independent African states. France certainly lacked business sense; Decca didn't have even an ounce of it. I should have copyrighted the song. What a fool—I hadn't believed in "Soul Makossa" enough myself.

To guarantee enough for Jerry and the band to stay alive on, I exhausted each of the usual clubs on my circuit in turn—the Caméléon, the Chevaliers du Temple. Sometimes I would go to Cameroon to play receptions financed by the banks or by fancy private-sector organizations. I needed more money. Coco and I had just moved into a pretty house in Joinville, and my ailing mother moved in with us. In one week, I created *Africadélic*—composing, arranging, and recording it. Its producer imposed a fifty-fifty split on me. The thing turned out to be a juicy affair—a veritable pension.

Makossa Man

Cash Box, one of the two American show-business bibles, ran an article on "Soul Makossa." The effect at Decca was nil. Rolande pushed, becoming the laughingstock of the company, but she didn't care. Like a cashier, she was in charge of the top-level bands pressed in Zaire and of raking in the profits, and the bosses gave her all the respect due a cashier. But she held fast to her certainty about the music while losing more and more money. Bad management. But she was stubborn. Her audacity was boundless, as was her sense of innovation. I will always be indebted to her; she reassured me and gave me confidence.

Suddenly, at the beginning of May, a lawyer phoned me from New York. The famous Ertegun brothers of Atlantic Records, the firm specializing in black music beloved by blacks as well as whites, were interested in little old me. "Soul Makossa" had already been so thoroughly pirated that it was time to pay attention to the real thing. The Erteguns wanted to work with me. I was lost; since Zéralda, I had been into soprano sax, very different in musical concept from the tenor style of "Soul Makossa." Rolande practically exploded; she convinced me. But Decca's directors were not going to let a woman in charge of the Africa division throw herself into a risky international operation. They were not hurting for money, and this sideline left them cold—all of them except one young wolf with long teeth who smelled something tasty. He didn't give a shit about black music, but the enormous amount of pirating that was happening in America called to him as a fine way to make the old company look fresh again and stand out. He persuaded the people at Decca to let him go to New York to see what he could turn up.

As soon as he arrived there, Warner, Capitol, and Atlantic contacted him. He negotiated with the Erteguns and came back with a plan for a contract with Atlantic. The two brothers heading that firm knew business. One of them, Ahmet, came personally to hear us at the Chevaliers du Temple. A divine surprise, as amazing as his assessment of us: in addition to the record, would we play at Harlem's Apollo Theatre, that temple of black music? Videotape and music videos did not yet exist. Ahmet made a rapid decision. He offered us a month-long tour in the United States with ten days at the Apollo. Now the Americans were in control of the game; Decca would show itself to be incapable of running the rest of the operation. Its leadership would have done better working in the Social Security Administration.

But I was in total fantasyland. My musicians were just as excited as I was. Who among us could have imagined such an adventure? Our feverishness jumped a notch. Every day we received word from over there. Our hit was big news. This would last as long as cut roses;

par for the course. American music critics called me for interviews.

As it happened, we discovered we'd been had in all this negotiating. We thought there was such a thing as a free lunch; as musicians, we were neither businessmen nor stars. The Erteguns had
planned for us to open for the Temptations. To them, as to Stevie
Wonder (then at their respective apogees), we were Africans who
looked American—an unknown species.

Smoke and mirrors. New York was moved by our African touch.
Why was "Soul Makossa" so popular? Crushed to pieces in Cameroon, appreciated in Zéralda, indifference in Paris. . . Why did the
U.S. ear like it so much? I would soon find out. The piece was released at the perfect moment. Afro wigs were all the rage. We felt as
if we were back home with the Zulus. The Americans appreciated
harmonies and vocal timbre close to their own. So what if they didn't
understand the meaning of the words? For them, "Soul Makossa"
evoked the Africa of the cities, the Africa they imagined when they
thought of the continent. Back home, people considered me European, and Europe treated me as an American. For Uncle Sam, I was
an African making African music.

In fact, it was no such thing. It was just a current, a component
I had managed to capture without respect for makossa's traditional
rhythm. I had stylized it according to my own lights, trailblazer that
I was (all modesty aside). My path made it clear that nontraditional
African music was possible. We can't recite our ancestors' lessons
forever; I hate recitals anyway. I'm a man between two cultures, two
environments; this is my destiny. "Soul Makossa" was the most out-
standing piece to have leapt from my loins. It would go around the
world because it expressed a huge emerging current. But, here again,
I hadn't known it. It was just my response to Louis Armstrong, who
knew how to humanize instrumentals and bring his difference to
bear on the common language. But the language must really be common to all for the public to understand each added contribution.

In the United States, "Soul Makossa" allowed people to begin
to explore African music. "Step after step, you are paying for your
good time," I sang in Douala. It hit your ears right; you didn't need
to understand the meaning. The publicity campaign took advantage
of the event. The Ertegun brothers announced our arrival: "The
first African musician is coming." This success would remain unequaled. It had to fall right on top of me . . .

Harlem in a Limousine

I couldn't believe my eyes when I set foot in New York. A swarm
of journalists hung on me, notified by Atlantic's promotion depart-
ment, which had put everything into it in order to get the most back.
It wasn't racist in that sense. Five limos carried us off. The entire
band was stupefied—the young wolf from Decca, Rolande, Coco,
Jerry, Slim Pezin, my two drummers (Claude Vamur and Lucien
Dobat), my Guadeloupean tumba player, and my Congolese singer.
We were led into a wild tornado. Staying at the downtown Hilton, I
was assailed by television stations. Every ten minutes someone was
knocking at my door to ask if I would give a five-minute interview.
Twelve stations, one right after the other. What a shock for us, coming from France, where there were only two!

Between two interviews, I got into a fight with Coco and the
manager. I wanted to perform "Soul Makossa" as I felt it now, not
as I had played it two years before. The jazz spirit in me rebelled at
the idea of repetition. My wife and the business team kept on at me;
I had to perform exactly what was on the record. I didn't know what
people saw in this record. I trusted my own feelings; I refused. Com-
plying with this commercial system would be like becoming a whore;
I'm not too good at that. In the past, when a mountain of diamonds
had passed under my nose in Zaire, I had been unaware of my own
good fortune. Since adolescence, I had gotten hung up on obstacles.
Aware of the importance of money, I erected endless castles in the
air with my crazy brain. When it came time to achieve them, I didn't
take step one.

So I imposed my own concept of how the band should be—no
brass as on the Yaoundé recording. The fateful Apollo tour date approached. Into our excitement was mixed the fear of opening for
our idols, the Temptations. We spent the week getting over jet
lag, practicing on-site to get familiar with the equipment. The adventure started to become real. We wandered around Harlem. Our
walks took us into history. This area looked a little like back home:
death was present, ordinary, almost natural. These reminiscences
relaxed us a little bit. We went around in a limousine. The blacks
celebrated us as heroes. Policemen asked me for autographs and for
the meaning of the words to "Soul Makossa."

Everything was going topsy-turvy inside my head. In one fell
swoop, I had arrived on U.S. soil, this country that until now I had
only fantasized about. It was a huge deal. The reality was equal to

what I had imagined from my reading. Nothing was missing from the myth. The Jazz Museum was near the Hilton and the Apollo—the temple of Duke Ellington, Count Basie, and all of my heroes.

Everything I had dreamed of was finally revealed to my gaze.

Africa at the Apollo

The curtain rose. In the wings, the Temptations entered the hall disconcertingly at ease. Used to the most famous stages, they paid us little attention. Hollywood was within reach, but we felt as though we were still on the other side of the divide. Fear caught in our throats. In the enormous hall, which also served as a movie theater, the crowd noisily waited for the show to open. I had never faced such a huge audience. I hardly dared cast a quick glance over these faces. Blacks, Puerto Ricans. I closed my eyes. Oh God, I felt sick! Africa was far away. *Nawedi wenge:* "I'm dead today, I'm dead," I murmured in Douala. For this audience, "Africa [had come] to Harlem." In their search for roots, these spectators had come to Manu Dibango. They had brought tambourines and maracas to celebrate Africa. In the first measures of "Soul Makossa," they went into a trance. They kept the beat. I had never seen such rhythm. Our good reception was guaranteed in advance, and I hadn't even known it. This wind of madness never let up through our ten days of concerts. The Apollo was a factory; we played twice a day, three times on weekends. During breaks, films were shown on a giant screen. When we got out of this effervescent lair, it was 2:00 A.M.

The barriers had been broken down. The Temptations, Johnny Pacheco (a Puerto Rican star), Barry White—people in the profession—applauded us and told us how much they respected us, in their typically direct way. Spanish Harlem and Black Harlem, whose relationship was often so conflicted, communicated their thanks to us in this mythical celebration of Africa. That was also an event. From it came contracts and trips that would fill the next two years of our lives. Travels across every continent resulted. I got a work permit and stayed in New York for two years. One of my cousins, Michel Doo-Kingué, an associate director at the UN, got me a diplomat's protected, comfortable apartment in a residential neighborhood. Coco appreciated the security.

From then on, people couldn't get enough of Manu Dibango. We gave a recital at Constitution Hall in Washington, DC. What a symbol! On our return to New York, I staggered under the most di-

verse commitments—television performances with black and white
groups; studio recording sessions (I had made a deal with Decca);
mixing and finishing an album begun in Paris in the worst conditions—*Makossa Man.* Decca's 24-track system was the first of its
kind and no one really knew how to use it. That was how I came to
make my first American recording. Balancing voices, choruses, vi-
braphones, and saxes was not easy. It all had to sound right to the
technicians' ears. We got used to their way of working. Between two
studio sessions, the director of Fania, the top label in Latin American
music, came to call. I was what he was looking for. We drew up a
contract for a tour with Johnny Pacheco and the Fania All-Stars in
Latin America and for a record and a film in Puerto Rico at the sites
where the slaves departed from. So much to look forward to . . .

One month after my gig at the Apollo, I gave a concert in Yankee Stadium—forty thousand people for this final evening before the
baseball stadium was to be renovated. Fear oozed from me again. Yet
I fit easily into the mindset and tempo. I thought I had pretty much
caught it, but I remained careful. I feared the consequences of the
fall that could result otherwise; I had done so much running around
in my adult life. I took advantage of it all, drunk on it. I felt as though
I was living in a dream from which I would awaken. The musicians
in the band were much cooler. They didn't hesitate to order French
wine in the best restaurants—they who didn't even drink wine before. The big bills were subtracted from my contract.

But Paris beckoned to me. One winter evening in 1973 I ran
back for my first date at the Olympia with Donna Hightower, an
American I had met in Brussels in 1960. The media saw me with
new eyes. I had successfully signed with Atlantic. It was rather more
gratifying than swimming in some dark corner of Decca's African
division. Before this feat, I had been hard to pin down, a musician
and not a singer.

After playing in the capital I went to Cameroon, where private
businessmen were holding their own festival. From Douala to Yaoundé via Garoua, with Coco, I was welcomed with prestige born
of my brand-new American renown. My compatriots respected me
without understanding too well why the American audiences had
been so excited about "Soul Makossa." The next generation would
understand that song better; their parents were unsure of the reasons
for my glory.

In January 1974, I participated in the MIDEM television festival
in Cannes. At the same time, I had been hired to compose the music

for a Nigerian film that was supposed to be shot in Lagos. I had to write the soundtrack in New York before going for the shoot. From Paris, I stopped over in Nigeria. The project came to nothing because of a political dispute, but I would use my songs in my upcoming records. I had formed a band with Americans for this recording, and now we didn't want to break up. We played the jazz circuit from one end of the United States to the other—the same clubs in which Miles Davis had performed. I was admired. The public was curious to see if I could handle their music. These musicians and I tried to "read" each other. Their perceptions interested me. I worked with many jazzmen who had already had famous hits. But our band did not manage to create a second "Soul Makossa." In spite of our failure, my good fortune did not abandon me: the impact of my favored song extended the world over. The Japanese produced a version of it, Brazilians copied it, and Parisian accordion players altered it to their tastes. Thanks to this hit, I jumped into show business with both feet; but since I had no support system, I didn't know how to manage my hit. I was in an unstable position, which I resolved by increasing my contracts.

New York was heating up over the fight of the century. Muhammad Ali's match against [George] Foreman. With other stars—James Brown, B. B. King, and the Fania All Stars—we went to Zaire, where the encounter took place. Millions of TV watchers were glued to their sets for the broadcast. I took advantage of the fallout from this event to promote *Makossa Man* on TV and radio, in newspapers and magazines.

Cameroon itself called me to a few festivities. I accepted with joy. In Yaoundé, I wrote a second version of "Soir au Village," composed ten years earlier. In 1964, its sales had never gone beyond about fifty copies, half purchased by me. This time, "Soir au Village" received applause. The change was noticeable: the fascination with the West that had followed close on the heels of independence had lessened a little. Institutions were in place now, and returning to one's roots had recovered its charm. Some people were even building weekend homes back in their villages. The words of my song evoked traditional gatherings over good grilled fish. The country discovered its artists and started to show them its appreciation, even if it didn't really understand their usefulness.

"Soir au Village" caught fire in Africa and also caught on in the Caribbean.

Afro-Music

The Fania tour started. I went alone, without the band. It was Manu who was invited, admitted into the great "family" of Latin American artists. Once a year, they got together to form the Fania All-Stars. These heavyweights would make a record together and go on a gala tour of Latin America for a month. Johnny Pacheco, Cheo Feliciano, Ray Barretto, Mongo Santamaria—Latin musicians I respected. Getting together to tour with them, U.S.–style, thrilled me. The major stop was in Puerto Rico. Its echoes resounded beyond the island. Caribbeans chartered planes to come to our concert. They did it for Manu. Then Caracas, Panama, and Miami followed, for crowds gone insane, comfortable in their luxury hotels. I came out of there stunned. I had earned a lot of money and been integrated into the "American way," all the while continuing my incessant traveling.

With money came a certain recompense: Hollywood nominated "Soul Makossa" and *O Boso*, the album it was on. Paris awarded me my first gold record with great pomp. I went to Cameroon to give this trophy to President Ahidjo—a step that would unceasingly be reproached as political. It seemed natural to me and symbolically translated the growing attachment I had to my roots. The president said he was proud of me, although he himself reproached me for not saying more strongly that I was Cameroonian. "I'm African," remained my refrain.

The meeting was intimidating, as the president took refuge in long silences. Since the international media were talking about me so much, why couldn't I be his personal public relations man, since he, Ahidjo, *was* Cameroon? I retorted, "None of your ministers has a budget that could pay for the publicity I've gotten my country in the United States." I tried a discreet suggestion: "Why not bring out a Cameroonian brand of coffee—Café Makossa? You'd sell tons of it over there." No answer. I emerged wounded from this experience. Clearly, artists still had to struggle to feel they had achieved real citizenship.

Coco didn't want to go with me. She took advantage of her stay in Paris to spend time with her own friends again, and she went to see her family in Brussels. Alone in Yaoundé, I went from party to party every evening. Adulation for me. Morality had degraded; here, sex was the national sport. With African logic, my son Michel was born as a result in 1976. In 1982, I would have another child this way, Marva.

My friends, those close to me, advised me to stay in the United States in the interests of my career. There I could really make my mark as an international musician. I didn't even consider it. The American way didn't satisfy my values or my roots.

One January morning in 1975, "luck" changed continents. I received a surprising call from Abidjan. A young wolf who had just made it as state information secretary had started Radio-Télévision Ivoirienne's national ensemble. I had the appeal of a media king; this guy had the money he needed for his project. He clearly planned to make a name for himself; he left no stone unturned. For me, he unfurled a long red carpet.

Côte d'Ivoire, Africa's pride. Sixteen years after my first visit to Abidjan, I continued along the path of my roots.

Agouti and *Foutou:*
Of Field Rats and *Fufu*

N EW YORK – PARIS – ABIDJAN in first class: my hosts
received me with the honors due a VIP. At the airport, TV
cameras filmed the event—an unheard-of celebration for a
French-speaking musician from sub-Saharan Africa. I wanted the
entire world to resound with the echo from my sax. A series of
concerts was planned. Abidjan spread its buildings and paved roads
out before me. The strides it had made were astounding. President
Houphouët-Boigny solemnly welcomed Coco and me to his residence at Cocody. He made me an honorary citizen. He gave me the
cloth wrap of a chief of the Baule—his ethnic group—before an
array of personalities, some of whose faces had been familiar to me
since my adolescent days on vacation in France.

The president was offering me the chance to become a cultural
catalyst. His deep desire was to reawaken self-love among his artists. Ivoirian traditional arts did exist, but not in music. Here, people
played in the Congolese, Nigerian, or Cameroonian style. The country didn't have one specific style; the weight of its ethnic groups
was a major obstacle. The president was working on the problem,
putting Ben Soumahoro, who was highly skilled in the audiovisual
domain, in charge of creating the ORTI, the Orchestre de la Radio-
Télévision Ivoirienne. The mission of this group would be to accompany artists invited from everywhere, no matter what their musical
language. The proposal was an enticing one: Abidjan already had
one national ensemble, the border police and army band. The new

group would enjoy special autonomy and even subsidy—extremely rare in Africa. But its ambition was not to serve warmed-over traditional music, thus ceding to the traditionalists' lobby. Not without difficulty, Ben Soumahoro had recruited musicians from Côte d'Ivoire and also from Ghana, Senegal, Nigeria, Zaire, Cameroon, and Mali. He had named as the leader of this Pan-African band Boncana Maïga, a Malian who had studied flute in a conservatory in Cuba. Ben had great plans for the band: high-powered evenings with guest artists and unusual live performances on radio and television, broadcast regularly to the general Ivoirian public.

Ben asked me to lead a workshop with the group for one week before the concert series began. Under the eye of the media, we had to make a big splash. The glow I had acquired in the United States from "Soul Makossa" was supposed to become the pride of the man in the street and of the highest official. We played amid high society at the Centre Cultural Français, in a boxing ring at Treichville (the neighborhood for black nightlife), and at the Bouake municipal pool. Our welcome was enthusiastic from both nationals and foreigners. Since I aspired to play for all different kinds of audiences in Africa, I was very glad.

Once back on African soil, I started to think over my American experience. In the United States, despite the hostility blacks endured—hostility that had at first scared me to the point that I didn't dare go down to buy a pack of cigarettes by myself—blacks were succeeding socially. Some were disc jockeys at influential radio stations; others were performers in that giant Western nation. From my own experience of two years there I drew real hope about the creative capacity of my brothers of color. The African system was not an insurmountable catastrophe. It could be reformed and could function more democratically than it currently did: as an all-powerful chief dominating a nonexistent herd. In Africa, a president could declare a man "competent" with one decree, than "incapable" with the next. The American example had convinced me that, with patience and goodwill, Africa would evolve by stages to a better future.

Thrilled with our concerts, Ben Soumahoro offered me leadership of the ORTI right away. I rejoiced, even though my nomination provoked displeasure from other quarters. Here I had been offered what Duke Ellington had always dreamed of—a stable band and the opportunity to work without financial constraints. This band of fifteen musician-singers I had been given was like modeling clay. Every bandleader's ambition was within my arm's reach: writing music for my own band, arranging and then hearing my discoveries immediately. My fabulous "instrument" incited me to compose for it and "play" it each time I felt the need. I could finally leave management troubles at the door; the musicians received a monthly salary paid by the government and I no longer had to concern myself with renting studios or recruiting musicians.

Ben Soumahoro's offer represented the realization of all my workshops. I went on the air each week. The whole country listened to me regularly. While gaining this listenership, I gained something else: I was able to accompany other artists who enriched me with their own repertoires. Clearly, this return to Africa was good for "Soul Makossa," I thought. I decided to move to Abidjan. I stayed for four years, as long as it took my incorrigible naïveté to tarnish greatly.

Paris's own Newport festival called together many jazzmen accustomed to the American festivals at the beginning of fall. I played wearing the traditional gown I had worn since my Apollo triumph. The Americans called me "Makossa Man." Paris celebrated me. Everybody wanted me. I could finally start up a project dear to my heart—a monthly musical magazine giving priority to African music, jazz, and popular music. *Afro-Music* featured a mix—an innovative notion in the business and one that would turn out to be ever so slightly precocious. Its avant-garde focus wouldn't become popular until the beginning of the eighties. For now, I invested all of my faith and no small amount of money in it. I love newspapers; wherever I am in the world, I run to the newspaper stands or beg papers from the bellboy. I need my fix—magazines from all over the world. I thirst for information. At home, after all, a musician is something of a journalist.

Afro-Music tried to be the link, the cement, for Africa's vast musical surge and for all the currents on the world scene. My travels had helped me understand all this wealth. The magazine was begun with the help of two journalists. Jean-Jacques Dufayet, a young manager at Decca who freelanced at RTL [a very popular radio station heard widely in France], soon became its editor in chief. The first issue came out in January 1977, the final one in October 1978. People liked it a lot, but few subscribed. When the cashbox was empty, *Afro-Music* ended.

"Qui Est Fou de Qui?"

Abidjan, October 1975: The rainy season had just ended when I officially took over direction of my band. The old leader had been fired, provoking discord within the band between his partisans and his adversaries. With complete serenity, I left them to quarrel. All that was important to me was that my musicians have an incredible amount of energy. Playing with me excited them. I was hard on them, faithful in this to my American experience. We had seven hours of rehearsal each day. My lessons bore fruit: in 1978, three years after our first encounter, the troupe triumphed from Congo to Morocco, even in Paris's famous Olympia concert hall. Later on, three members would join Alpha Blondy's band at the start of his career.

Coco and I stayed at the Hôtel Ivoire, the best in the city, as guests of the state. I seemed to be a president's man; I didn't recognize the trap set for me. Over the course of weeks, Ben Soumahoro came under fire. His strong character had offended more than a few. "That guy is really mean," people said of him. The hard reality was impossible for me to bear; I refused to hide my feelings under a tough, inaccessible shell. In the future, I would understand that I was just not made to live in Africa. Fax, the one who had owned the Tabou in Brussels—good old Fax with his famous trumpet—had come home, and he ran a small club. He enjoyed the respectful nickname of "Patriarch" without being given a dime of pension. Cruel treatment.

But Abidjan showed off its fineries and temptations to "Manu" during this period of 1975. I was the president's protégé and Ben Soumahoro's prize horse. Brutally, Ben came under the rule Africa imposes on those who would command. He was not admired; he was respected out of fear. He was a Muslim who neither drank nor smoked—unassailable at that level. He had confidence in me. In this, he was the one who defended my record to his minister, who was stumbling under the most outrageous demands. My reception by the president made my nascent collaboration with Ben easier. Euphorically I composed "Qui Est Fou de Qui?" ["Who's Mad for Whom?"], a symbolic title that my musicians found hilarious.

The good vibes soon faded. On 13 January 1976, my father died in Douala. At the time I was in Cannes for the MIDEM festival, accompanied by part of the Yaoundé police band, with which I had just recorded an album, *Manu 76*. In record time—two days—the

Cameroonian government had agreed to put these musicians at my disposal. In the time it took to catch a plane, I left Cannes to bury my father in Douala. Seven months later, on 13 August, I was in Abidjan when I learned of my mother's sudden death. The next day President Houphouët-Boigny received me, as the African father he could be. Ivoirian radio and television interrupted their broadcasts to announce my mother's death.

As serious as differences are in Africa, the continent is able to respect human life and dignity—under certain circumstances. I was even more shocked when at the end of that same week the manager of the Hôtel Ivoire called on me with no consideration and said, "Monsieur Dibango, you have to pay your bill; the television station can't pay, since the minister said not to." I talked to Ben Soumahoro. "No problem," he reassured me. He loaned me a studio apartment belonging to his wife while we waited to find housing. Here we were stuck for three months in a tiny, humid room. Coco was sick about it. We couldn't receive guests; the place was even more uncomfortable since we had just adopted Georgia. She is of my own blood, daughter of one of my cousins. We had watched over her since her birth in Cameroon. Georgia is mixed-race; she is the child God gave Coco and me. As we were now stably situated in Abidjan, we took her on with us permanently.

"Afrique sans Fric"

Our cargo finally arrived by boat. I got my Mercedes back. Sidewalk radio couldn't keep from talking: "Houphouët-Boigny himself gave it to Manu." A wind of calumny drifted in. Here, artists were used to living on alms and gifts given by the patriarch. The president was God, and God is good. You just had to go see him to complain that you didn't have working materials, and he would release five million CFA francs. I refused to compromise myself in this way. The idyllic picture I'd painted for my partner dimmed before our eyes. Coco, who had already tasted Africa's bitter charms, saw new disasters on the horizon. The situation worsened a little more when an underhanded disagreement with my musicians arose.

They accused me of eating the Ivoirians' *foutou*—that is, their bread. This staple is made from manioc flour and is called *fufu* in Cameroon. All Africans have to withstand history's weight: they can accept a white man providing technical assistance to them, but not a black man. As an African, I was to be rejected by all of Abidjan and treated like an *agouti*, the field rat people enjoyed in Treichville's back-street restaurants. People didn't tell me directly; jealousy prefers its wicked trickery.

Here people are very good chemists, possessing the ability to poison a person. They can execute you more smoothly than did anyone in Florence: even an autopsy won't show the African poison hidden under your nails. Now we had to be careful—we had cans of beer or bottles of wine opened right in front of us. We never knew from which corner danger might come. In Africa, you don't die; you're "sold" to an evil spirit.

Ben Soumahoro himself knew something of this. His guru, Kante, a famous Guinean journalist, was in political exile in Côte d'Ivoire. He was also a Muslim and of the same ethnic group as Ben. Their professional value was recognized, but their ambition was frightening to the artistic world: they had dared to select a Malian as the first bandleader, and then they had kicked him out to bring in a Cameroonian. Jealousy compounded jealousy. I went from the frying pan into the fire—lots of fun. I had always defended the idea of a single Africa; I found out instead that there are Africa*s*. Either model is all right, provided it works. But what a disappointment! Coco thought I was walling myself off in my Africanness. This was true, and I did so willingly because I had thought I could be useful here—more so than in Cameroon, which had neither national television nor the desire to create a musical renaissance. Back home was where I had known fear as a child; in Abidjan, I didn't have that feeling. Now I knew that in Africa you have to be clear in your head or you're soon destroyed psychologically.

Ben Soumahoro, his Guinean guru, and I were firm in our solidarity. Since Georgia needed to get to school and Coco was sick, we had to leave that unhealthy studio. I resolved to beg for a meeting with the president. Through his influence, Ben obtained a meeting. We went together. Ben told the president about my role and my needs. Houphouët-Boigny agreed and gave Ben a mandate to find me a new house. The task was no easy one: an appropriate villa rented for a lot of money—about ten thousand francs per month. The president would pay the bill. Sidewalk radio rumors thickened: "The president is housing Manu." A new trap. Houphouët-Boigny had his reasons. He painted himself as a peasant who had made good, and he wanted to enjoy the same kind of international intellectual recognition as Senghor, who sat on the Académie Française. He liked the arts and adored boxing, but he was neither a poet nor a musician. For Houphouët-Boigny I was useful, and, in the same way, someone to sacrifice as soon as the need arose. The notoriety I had acquired with "Soul Makossa" would cost me a lot. I found myself on the front lines and fought the fires.

Despite low blows, I composed relentlessly. Jealousy bred and grew stronger. My many contracts were like swords stuck into my enemies' sides. I wrote the soundtrack for *L'Herbe Sauvage*, a film produced by Côte d'Ivoire and directed by Henri Duparc, who would later give us *Bal Poussière*. I took advantage of a visit to Paris to write the music for some publicity spots for the African market—a first achieved by Ben, who was able to sell the commercial merits of the young ORTI. In return for payment from French public relations agencies, I bragged musically about the qualities of certain beer, soap, and cloth. When I did so, I called in musicians with whom I had worked in Paris to accompany me. My colleagues in Abidjan felt furiously resentful toward me: "A Cameroonian can do commercials, but not we Ivoirians?" The ones in the Ensemble National or at the Institut des Arts were the most ferocious, having obtained their positions through connections and trickery (because they belonged to a certain ethnic group or were a minister's cousin). They didn't have the ability of the army band members, who could read music perfectly and who knew "classical" standards because of their training in the French army. Of course, it was not the *French* who had taught them to swing!

This lack of musical education was precisely what dictated the brave step I took on my return to Abidjan: "If you're going to pay for training, send them to the United States or bring in black American professors of recognized ability. That would be a step forward." My goal to be a precursor incited no comment; it was simply and completely ignored. Later, musicians in the Cameroonian army would make successful records; the administration protected and paid them but also pocketed the royalties that I thought should have gone to the artists themselves, who had such a hard time surviving.

"Afrique sans Fric" ["No-Cash Africa"]—I wrote it inspired by just these kinds of injustices and anomalies. The traditionalists of the Ensemble National cast a bitter eye on me. Their intrigues achieved the desired end: the difference of opinion became political. Criticisms of me embarrassed Soumahoro and soon the president himself. I was clearly someone to sacrifice because I posed a basic problem as an African technical assistant.

I still had a few good times left to enjoy. Bokassa was getting ready to have himself crowned emperor, and he demanded the presence of a great band for the ceremony. The ORTI was invited. I was told the happy news in Cameroon, where I was visiting. On leaving Abidjan, the presidential plane was to stop at the Yaoundé airport to pick me up. At the agreed-upon time I went there and mentioned to the employees that I was waiting for a plane. "There isn't one in the afternoon," they told me nonchalantly. "Yes, there is!" "We don't know about it." "What? It was supposed to be here at three o'clock this afternoon." The air police grew disturbed. I was still there with my sax when a plane appeared on the horizon, making its descent. Its eruption on the scene almost provoked a diplomatic incident. It didn't have permission to land, and moreover it was full of Ivoirian ministers. Jealous tongues talked up this event too: "A plane coming from Abidjan just to pick up one passenger!" After all the palaver and a multitude of contradictory opinions, the plane was authorized to land and then return to its path to Bangui, capital of the Central African Republic.

The ORTI, "Father" Houphouët-Boigny's band, was received with respect. Money flowed like water. The church was sumptuously decorated. Among the guests was Michel Droit, the academician, who was seated right in front of me. At the end of the service, golden carriages were brought for a solemn parade led by flower-bedecked horses. That evening by moonlight we were giving our concert when a violent storm suddenly erupted; the carriages were soaked, the projectors broke down, the musicians got drenched. The dignitaries thought only of hiding themselves in their Mercedeses. We found ourselves alone, the horses and us, awaiting the clemency of the skies. Farewell, carriages. We needed our fee. Bokassa kept the keys to the locked safe on his person; a coup d'état can happen so quickly. After a long wait I was taken to the safe, where our fee was removed.

Round-trips to Lagos came frequently. In one hour by plane, I could get to Fela and his friends. Lagos had an ultramodern recording studio. Around 1978, I succeeded in bringing out one of my best albums, *Home Made*. I rehearsed in Calabar with Nigerian and Ghanaian musicians for a week and a half before the studio session. In Nigeria, it received the first gold prize ever given a recording by a foreigner. A few months after this record's success, I went to Paris to play the Olympia, and then to Jamaica.

Abidjan

Back home, the ORTI got back to work. We had plans for a month-long tour—an innovation on the continent—beginning in Brazzaville, continuing in Morocco, and closing in Paris. Our manager was the one who usually organized Claude François's and Johnny Hallyday's African tours. We were to be accompanied by The Love Machine, a Los Angeles band famous for its dancers, who were as beautiful as they were talented. We numbered forty all together and had three tons of equipment. We also lacked nothing in naïveté.

After much labor, our project received the necessary official authorization. I no longer had complete confidence in Ben Soumahoro, who was shaken by the extent of the jealousy against me. Sidewalk radio again unleashed a torrent about me, serving me up in all kinds of jealous stories. The Ivoirian media didn't want to cover me, but the artistic director of the ORTI demanded my presence. He saw the opportunity to show off with this African tour; my reputation served him well. We left Côte d'Ivoire. The curious atmosphere made me feel like a fifth wheel. The fire driving me had died. I was hurt, even somewhat wounded, by this rise of hatred. I satisfied myself with the passion of making music, but the Ivoirians were insensitive to it. They saw me first as a foreigner. I had enjoyed living among Ivoirians so much in my youth that this reaction from the people of Abidjan broke my heart.

The tour was nonetheless a success. We closed brilliantly in Paris, where we played at the Olympia. Would Côte d'Ivoire appreciate us? Alas! On our return, we had hard times. I became fully aware of the grave differences between me and my enemies. I was becoming a burden to Houphouët-Boigny, who hadn't stopped paying my rent. Coco and I discussed the matter seriously, and I decided not to ask for the renewal of my lease. I admit to leaving Côte d'Ivoire without seeing its president again, and with no explanation. I moved Coco and Georgia to Paris and prepared to fly to Jamaica alone to record a double album.

The last years I had lived in Côte d'Ivoire taught me profoundly about Africa—a bitter discovery. Since I wasn't a civil servant, I couldn't work there. What good was my reputation if I was obliged to run around to presidents for money? Awareness is painful. Africa does not tolerate freedom of creation in music. This means that elsewhere—in other sectors—the same obstacles are also the rule. This is a fact: intellectuals who return home don't use their abilities. Artistic creativity is under close surveillance. I once saw our real motherlode, our real cash crop, in creativity. I still think this, but Abidjan greatly diminished my optimism. Artists, like athletes, have to leave the continent to practice their profession. Their success is not Africa's; it is due only to their own strong individualism. They are condemned to remain freelancers. Ten years later, this reality hasn't changed an iota. Without an infrastructure for its artistic industry, Africa loses money every time Manu sells a record on his own soil! It's too much. A royalty-collecting structure will one day be put in place for artists, but its funds will disappear in smoke, without anyone knowing what happened to the profits. Artists will have to wait for years before getting their fees. Touré Kunda and Mory Kanté are not children of Africa; it is France that helped them get started.

In fact, every time I dream of Africa, with her fantasies and plans, she is a source of disillusionment and wounding. My long stay in Côte d'Ivoire turned me into one of those people who has a pain in his Africa.

Paris now seemed a harbor of tranquility. Coco and Georgia were at peace. Disoriented, I prepared to confront the distant, unknown landscapes of Jamaica.

"Douala Sérénade"

ON THE ISLE OF THE RASTAS, my blues evaporated under reggae's caresses. This was the first encounter between Africa and Jamaica. The warm, electric, sensual atmosphere reinvigorated the man who had abandoned Abidjan, his heart heavy with disappointment. The vitality of Jamaican rhythms fed my inspiration. I had prepared only three songs for this requested album, but I felt so good that compositions flowed naturally from me. Though I had come for a week, my stay extended to a month. We recorded a double album with the evocative title *Gone Clear*. Now the skies were clear; the sorrows of past days had dissipated in musical happiness. *Gone Clear* breathed. It called me to find my place again, my place as a musician. The Jamaicans surprised me, lighting little lamps of creativity. We recorded every afternoon. In the morning, I would go to Bob Marley's. He showed me his studio, his talent, and his ways of working.

When the month had elapsed, I went to the United States to incorporate brass, strings, and voices into our recordings—four weeks in the studio. *Gone Clear* turned out to be an expensive product, but it was worth it. Georgia and Coco came with me on this trip. "Luck" returned to me. These three months softly distanced me from my African tensions.

"Doctor Bird"

We returned to Paris in October 1979. My cousin-brother put us up until we found the right apartment. Then my little family moved

into the area around the Père Lachaise Cemetery, where you'd almost think you were in the country. That part of the twentieth district in Paris gives off its own brand of village bonhomie. Georgia
liked her school; Coco recovered her health. Paris gave us back our
peace. It was our final harbor, we hoped. Since the age of fifteen, I
had moved around Paris every time I returned from one continent
or another. I've never felt like a foreigner there. Returned from my
trials, strong with my successive triumphs and failures, I was becoming a Parisian African, a mutant species. The African traveler passing
through Paris had given way to the Afro-European.

Now I began with nothing. Once again, I started up a band. But
the thing I had for my homeland caught up with me again. Côte
d'Ivoire had rejected me because I was a foreigner, but in Cameroon, it would be different; I would be at home. Little by little, self-
persuasion made its inroads. I went more and more frequently to
Yaoundé for "one-shot" deals; once there, I would set up bands. I
had one foot in Paris and my fantasies in Cameroon. Back home,
one of my close friends, a doctor in philosophy, had just been named
minister of culture. His ambition was as great as it was sincere. Cameroonian music was beginning to be felt across the continent; all
of Africa was dancing to makossa. My friend and I preferred not
to weigh ourselves down with the individualist's yoke; we wanted to
forge a unified image of Cameroon, representing all the musical currents in the country. We brought together about twenty artists, from
traditional to religious to bar music. This notion resulted in a three-
record set, *Fleurs Musicales du Cameroun* [*Musical Flowers of Cameroon*].

I believed that this was the project that would finally let me
make a success of my relationship with Africa. But the project caused
me mountains of agony from its conception. Out came those old
jealousies again. Out of two thousand artists we considered, we chose
only twenty—which gave us a hell of a lot of enemies. The elect
themselves balked at being selected and lamented that only one of
their pieces had been chosen. My friend was unbending under these
attacks, solid as a rock. At the same time, he started a cultural magazine, *Afouacom*.

A few years before in Yaoundé I had met Hervé Bourges,
founder and then-director of the Ecole Camerounaise de Journalisme, who later became the CEO of the French TV station TF1 and
then of Radio Monte Carlo. We now became friends forever. He
opened my mind to politics and great causes. Another Yaoundé lu-
minary in this period (the beginning of the eighties) was a childhood

friend whose father was one of the wealthiest men in Cameroon. He had wanted to be a musician: he had the fiber of a businessman and adored music. He, too, had his own ideas, and he took me along on his dream. His father had a hotel in Douala, and my friend wanted to open an international nightclub there. He begged me ardently: "The club will shake up this city; all it's ever known are those little port bars. Once a month, we'll bring in famous foreign artists. You'll take care of that part."

"This job," he told me, "won't take up all your time, and you can continue shuttling back and forth between Paris and Cameroon." This time, Coco refused to follow me to Douala. She knew the film by heart, and she didn't plan to stay around to watch it again. Since my parents' deaths in 1976, she had remained firm in her position. She told me over and over again that my returning to Africa was just a fantasy. Once more, I didn't believe her, at least not yet. In Yaoundé, my son Michel had just turned six.

Douala was my home away from home. I had a house there—my parents' home—and a mission of national importance to fulfill. My pockets were full, thank goodness, because my life-style called for lots of money. The Japanese firm Toyota had pressed me into service for its car campaign in Africa, where the Corolla model was coming out. I signed a contract, and they financed a tour with a troupe of twenty-five people in return for one record, "MakossaToyota-Corolla." The kids got the records for free, and you could hear them singing the song—loudly enough to break your eardrums—in all the streets of the continent. The thing was so big that cab drivers in Yaoundé and Douala called me a two-timer if I allowed myself to be driven in anything other than a Toyota. These cabbies drove Toyotas. "Too bad for Peugeot or Renault," I told a French manager I met at a cocktail party shortly after my arrival in Yaoundé. "The Japanese wanted to corner the market. They shelled it out, and even rented a plane for my tour. French companies are resting on their monopolies."

Seen as the Toyota man, I was utterly confident. I threw myself body and soul into my new battle. This trial of truth would be my last African adventure. Of course, as always, I didn't see it coming.

"Mboa"

Douala, fall 1981: "Mboa"—"at home" on the wings of a song. The instruments I had carefully, personally chosen in the best Parisian shops finally arrived at the right port. I had even bought a Hammond organ, planning for the trios and quartets I wanted to invite to the future club. A little band wouldn't be too expensive. Soon our cabaret opened its doors with great pomp. The concept was excellent, but its operation quickly became burdensome. We had no discounted plane tickets, no money to install the soundproofing we needed, and little resistance to the "neighborhood business" that inevitably grafted onto our work. Figures in hand, we had to admit that our operation was obviously not profitable. Yet we drew such a high-class audience. I managed to bring in a pianist I really believed in, Jean-Claude Naimro, who later became Kassav's pianist. I even gave him the chance to bring out a record on Afrovision, one of the three labels I had created back home in the past few years.

Our Douala club, with its international aspirations, was a bottomless pit that devoured us. It finally closed its doors after running for six months. Perhaps Jean-Claude Naimro had made money in Douala, but I had lost a lot, and it was not over yet.

My friends in Yaoundé tried to tell me that the capital had a wider audience. "The students and expatriates are bored. Maybe you could amuse them." They bragged about the merits of a luxurious restaurant that had been set up in a fancy apartment building. "You have to open a club there. The need is there. You could get subsidized." To my mind, the time had come to open a place where people could go to listen to this famous Cameroonian music heard everywhere but in Cameroon. Here local artists could express themselves in dance, music, and skits to delight my compatriots. A national television station was going to start up in accordance with the government's wishes. I hoped to keep its shows supplied with the artists I would invite to the club. Finally, the place would acquaint local musicians with the big names on the world music scene.

My friends in Yaoundé decided to invest in my name and my responsibility. But in reality, they didn't keep their financial promises. Faced with their pulling out, I could only place my hopes in those famous subsidies, which turned out to be hypothetical. On the day I had planned to open the head of the construction crew warned me that the air-conditioning couldn't be run at night. No one had thought to tell me, and since the building was only four years old, there was no way for me to guess that we might have this problem. So off I went, looking for fans.

The club's inauguration unfolded with ministers but without air-conditioning. Me—spend ten million CFA francs to equip the club? No way. Despite my troubles, success didn't wait to come. To the hall decorated like the Don Camilo (a famous Paris cabaret) all Yaoundé came to dine and watch the show. Rhoda Scott, now a rising star, came to play the organ for a week. A woman at the organ—they had never seen that here! It was a real event.

But my clientele aroused bad feeling and envy. Those "local things," the traditional ones, made their way into my club. It was very strange: my enemies brought African "medicine" into the club to dissuade my clientele from coming in.

Black Magic

One evening when I was just returning from Paris I ran over to the club. My foot hit something sticking out. An air pocket? Had the costly rug come unstuck already because of the humidity in the air? Or had it simply been badly laid? I continued walking to the bar, and again my foot hit something. I looked, lifted up the corner of the rug, and discovered balls wrapped in cloth. What could they contain? I asked the servant boy to open them. As soon as I did, my words gave him wings. He fled; he didn't want to touch them. He knew what they were. All the rest of the staff knew what they meant, all except me. I remained aghast. Tension overtook the musicians. The city learned from sidewalk radio that "they've given Manu medicine."

From this point on, the local people didn't come to the club. Some expatriates braved the danger, but I lost an incredible amount of money. I had requested credit, and I had to honor my debts. I hung on and decided to start living here, going to see Georgia and Coco from time to time. My heart was torn between France, where my wife and Georgia lived, and Cameroon, where my son Michel and my daughter Marva lived. Telephone connections were a problem. To get my own line, I rented a luxurious villa, a real cement house. I lived alone in this too-big space.

Scarcely a month after the incident with the balls came a second and disastrous incident. One dark night after coming home from the club, I went to the toilet to read my newspaper. A moment of lovely quiet passed. The surrounding calm relaxed me. I was getting up off the seat when I saw a green snake, the kind whose bite means death. Unfortunately the telephone still wasn't connected. The villa was far from the center of town. Was I going to die here, so absurdly? How could I get out of this with just my shoes and pants? But it was

decidedly not my time to go. I didn't delay reacting. I took my first
slipper and held it out to the snake so he would bite it and release
his venom. Then I could leave. I took off my second slipper. The
reptile still had his head up. Slowly I took off my pants and threw
them on him. I stepped over him, opened the door carefully, and
closed it again. Early in the morning, the houseboy killed the snake.
Its venom had already burned the cloth of my pants.

The next day was a memorable Monday. I went down to Douala
to see my mother's sister. She had asked a friend from a village in
the bush who didn't speak French to lunch with us. This woman had
ability as a seer, and she started telling me about my recent mis-
adventures. There was no way she could have known in advance.
Her somber prophecies frightened me. "People are creating a lot of
vibrations on you. You will have to deal with a snake again. You need
to be brave, because it will be very hard." What kind of curse was I
under that I couldn't create something here in Cameroon? If there
were any logic in all this, my mind could deal with it. Confronted
with those "local things," I had no effective weapon to defend myself. I completely lost my head.

I called Coco. "I told you not to go back to Africa," she said.
She wrote to me, "You'd do more for Africa far away from her."
Then again, on the phone: "I'm coming to see you." Crazed, I
dashed to Douala to welcome her. I asked a nephew to bring my
Toyota from Yaoundé to Douala at the appointed time. The car
never got there; as it arrived in the city, it had a serious accident. A
car ran into it for no reason. Its driver was an influential civil servant,
a surveyor with whom I was negotiating for some land. How could
I fight him, or even get an honest evaluation of what had happened
from the police? I had no proof. And Coco concluded, "You see,
every time you achieve something, an obstacle crosses your path. On
balance, you're always the loser. Why not give up Africa to return
to France? You've given enough." Since 1957, the year we met, Coco
had been my guardian angel. She had confronted mistrust and dis-
like, the pitfalls Africa can hold for foreigners.

Around me the real world, the spirit world, and the sorceror's
world mingled. The air was unbreathable. I was reeling from my
debts, millions of francs to be reimbursed. These debts I took on and
paid off over many years. I left Cameroon with my body and my soul
raw, with my deepest wound: it was my home I was fleeing.

I had a hard time healing from this nightmare. I was sick for
a long time because of Cameroon. Thank God my children Michel

and Marva have helped me keep my emotional ties to my country. In this dark night, one certainty came through loud and clear: I didn't have it in me to be a businessman. Everything I had tried at home had failed. I made lots of money playing and wasted it on fantasies. Was I on the wrong path? Not completely—since my departure from Cameroon, supper clubs have flourished there. Later on, some young artists would become famous at these kind of places, groups such as Les Têtes Brûlées and Essindi Mindja. In fact, my plans had made sense.

This time, I returned to Paris for good. The page was turned forever. At least, so I thought. The misunderstanding between me and my country was a basic one. I'm beloved in Cameroon as long as I'm not there: "I love you even more when you're not here."

"Pour une Poignée de CFA"

I was back in Paris's twentieth district, under the peaceful shadow of Père Lachaise. This time, unfortunately, I didn't feel as though I had returned to the fold. Too much confusion and bitterness haunted me. I tried to see clearly. The future of my country worried me. I continued in my failure to understand any of it. Years of independence have gone by. What seed have the successive governments planted in people's heads? The kids don't believe school is useful because their fathers can buy them their diplomas. The god Money is master everywhere. People will do anything for a fistful of CFA francs, as I have said in my song. The idea of the commonweal is nonexistent. People take great care of their villas and forget the edifice they were building for the nation. They build post and telephone offices without planning for the phone booths. A budget is voted on to widen a road; someone stints on twenty centimeters the whole of its length to put more money in his pocket. No one *earns* money; everyone just knows how to use it. The dice are loaded. "Black Africa has gotten off to a bad start," the French Green Réné Dumont wrote; in fact, she may not take off during this century. While this analyst poses the problem at an economic level, I feel it in terms of more serious obstacles: Africa is having trouble finding herself.

After the colonialists left, Africa gained a margin in which to maneuver. But the whites still have some of their power, which they now exercise differently. How can Africa take over the empty margin? Everything is done to impress the onlookers. Do you have a nice house? It's empty, soulless, because it was built with no heart. There's the rub. Is my thirst for love Western or African—or simply ethical? I don't know anymore.

To succeed, I was condemned to be an expatriate. Members of the next musical generation will have to leave the continent en masse to get their place in the sun. Back home, freedom is costly; in fact, the price hasn't even been set yet. When will this flight come to an end? We can't accuse whites forever . . .

When Africa talks of ethics, it advocates a return to roots. This is a facile solution that goes nowhere. I would accept it if it opened up a new path. We have never left our roots. Like all continents, Africa has its past; like others, it has been colonized. That time is over. Creativity is our only path to health—making way for the imagination.

"Négropolitain"

Stuck in my contradictions, I suffered deeply. This story without end looked like a record turning—until a frail light went off in my head. Back home, I could talk openly: the cat never had my tongue; I had never kept from talking. I had a unique ability to put my foot in my mouth, regardless of the rank of the person listening to me. Why admire this or that dignitary who could do nothing to enrich my artistic sensibility? During my life as a musician, I had always been nourished by my encounters. But it was pointless to drive myself crazy as if, like Tintin, I had a special mission to accomplish back home. In Cameroon, no one cared; they were all too involved in their wheeling and dealing. So Tintin went into exile, to general indifference.

Once I accepted this obvious piece of information, I began to feel better. I would continue to pay off my debts and return to being a musician—my real profession. My own world is Charlie Parker, John Coltrane, Louis Armstrong, Hugh Masekela, and the Africa I keep in my head.

"Tam-Tam Pour L'Ethiopie"

PARIS, JUNE 1982. Was it the return of the prodigal son? Not quite. I returned to my home, my family, and habits acquired in this city, obligatory stopping place on all my many trips. Seeing me lost, Coco took me under her wing and served as my manager. She loved music, knew the jazz milieu, and "sold" me with all the stubbornness of a Capricorn. Anticipating my arrival, she had already knocked on several doors. The club Jazz Unité had opened up in the Défense area, and the owners were ready to purchase a few of my evenings if I could get a band together. Coco had gotten the OK of our friends in Belgium, hastily contacted after our long silence. We held several concerts there.

Coco got busy. Her name spread among the expatriate Africans of Paris. This was how Mamadou Konté entered into my life. For four years, he had organized the Africa Fête at the Porte de la Villette, an annual gathering of the avant-garde and the jumping-off point for the Africans of Paris. Mamadou had a political activist's background. He asked me to participate in Africa Fête 1982, where I met those who became my daily companions.

These exiles had arrived with nothing. These isolated, broke musicians with no papers would transform Paris into a world capital of African music. They were French-speaking. Their English-speaking counterparts—such as Fela, a Nigerian from Lagos, and his Afro-Beat—preferred to remain in their own countries while forging their careers.

In this rich soil, a handful of French people played the gardeners.

They tried unusual means. The spirit of this movement tied us very closely together. No matter that I knew more about African problems than they, with their scarcely realistic visions; their passion revealed unseen talents, a new sound that no one would have suspected without their help. Like an explorer, Martin Messonnier was on the lookout for seeds that would germinate. Gilbert Castro and François Post helped them grow at Celluloid, their production house. Rémy Kolpa-Kopoul and Philippe Conrath at *Libération*, Jean-François Bizot at *Actuel*, and Jean-Jacques Dufayet and Sylvie Coma at Radio France Internationale realized which way the African wind was blowing. They were inseparable from this newly expatriate generation of African individualists: Ray Lema from Kinshasa, who was exploring the secrets of electronic composition adapted to his roots after pursuing traditional rhythms far into the bush with his tape recorder. Mory Kanté from Guinea, who walked about with his griot's kora, trained in the Mandingo tradition. Salif Keïta from Mali, who dared to defy custom: a lord's son, he sang like a griot with his golden voice and albino allure. The three Touré brothers from Casamance, who were trying out a Broadway-style stage setting for their ancestral rhythms. Alpha Blondy, the Ivoirian rastafarian, who disturbed and fascinated with his challenging chants; his "Brigadier Sabari" knew no borders. Xalam, the group from Dakar, whose members mixed a jazz tempo and the rhythms of their land into their rock.

The ground had been planted for a growth of a real cultural current that was no longer exotic in the least. Mamadou was its catalyst; I was very likely its precursor. Ultimately, this generation's arrival reassured me: people like me were not doomed to be "accidents." My success had proved that an African could get by without compromising. On the path of the patriarch, their arrival as musical guerrillas was the start of what was likely to become a movement. In France, a leftist government had just come to power. Hervé Bourges and Jack Lang, then minister of culture, threw down the gauntlet by subsidizing several concerts. The "empty-bellies" could make enough money to keep on composing.

Cameroon invited me to perform a few times. I played for several days, but the umbilical cord had been cut. Hervé Bourges put me in charge of getting together the band for a meeting of African leaders in Vittel [France]. This was a responsibility that suited me: my band was both white and black, Catherine Lara side by side with Touré Kunda. The concert was broadcast for television. The Touré brothers' show revealed their rising star. They were the first African group to think about *directing* their musical performance. From them I learned how to introduce the aspect I was lacking: the showmanship appropriate to the times. I tended to think more narrowly about how a concert should go. But they said there should be no music without dancing, in the hall or on stage. Jack Lang got into Touré Kunda. Colleagues of the Tourés found work in their wake. On this foundation, and in the delights of drunken nights, the world of African music was put in place in Paris. Vittel's echoes called us to more ambitious projects.

The Talking Tree

Hervé Bourges got me off to a good start. He breathed the sense of a cause into me. Through him, I entered into politics in my own way, more humanitarian than political. Up to this point, I had done nothing more than being in the same place at the same time as the major upsets following the African independences. In his soul a friend of the Third World, Hervé Bourges forced me to go beyond the petty quarrels and to open myself to new horizons. The light dawned. I went to Holland for a concert intended to raise funds for Ethiopia, where severe famine was raging. When I returned to Paris, I called on Martin Messonnier, with whom I had just produced a record, "Abele Dance," to American and British acclaim. I shared my idea with Martin: "We should try to do here what they did in Holland." Martin responded, "You think so? I'll talk to Philippe and Rémy." The idea for a 45 took shape. But who would release it? Constantin at Virgin, the British firm dominating the market, obtained Phonogram-Philips's approval. We got a studio, but we needed musicians. Our little circle had faith. We shared the work. The French guys took on the task of contacting the right officials; I contacted Bourges and African musicians.

Alpha Blondy entered the picture. At my house, we sought a melodic framework on piano and synth that we could show the others. The royalties would go to Médecins sans Frontières [Doctors Without Borders]. During our conversation, I brought up Salif Keïta's name. Alpha became furious: "It's either him or me; if it's him, I'm out." I retorted, "Leave your ego at the door!" Alpha slammed the door. I hadn't known that there was such hatred between them, the result of an amorous rivalry. Salif and then Mory Kanté gave their OKs. The Touré brothers had to be persuaded. It was as though we were back at home, under the talking tree, seated around the local chief. The Touré brothers were at the top of the Paris scene; the idea would be best coming from them. Rémy Kolpa-Kopoul, who was close to them, used his Levantine diplomacy to convince them. We also wanted Miriam Makeba's collaboration. Her manager, a daft Swiss, didn't understand the importance of our project: "If there's no money to be made, Miriam won't budge." Hugh Masekela, whom I admired, was in Botswana and couldn't participate in our enterprise in person, but I offered him a deal: we would record his voice by phone and mix it later. The same scenario for a paralyzed Zairian female singer. People telephoned from all over the place. What a fantastic challenge!

We had a first: gathering all these artists whose tempers were as fickle as they could be gloomy for a single song. "Tam-Tam pour l'Ethiopie" ["Tam-Tams for Ethiopia"] was one big trip across Africa, from west to south. Each of us had to feel at ease in this piece, and each got a certain number of measures. We had to find the right rhythm to carry it all: a bass line, a drum line, and a space for each voice that allowed all of us to express ourselves. For once we did better than the Americans without expending their kind of money. Télé Libé TV made a spot from it. "Tam-Tam pour l'Ethiopie" was a pioneering piece that made the Top 50. Here, then, was proof that Africans too could take concrete action. I had always dreamed of it; I was thrilled.

In Mory Kanté's company, I went to Ethiopia. We took the funds resulting from the record's sales into the refugee camps. For once, the money wouldn't be misused by the government in power. The evening of our arrival in Addis Ababa we were invited to a cocktail party, a real blow-out. I got the heaves. Our visit to the camp was not planned, and it was disconcerting to some people. With the TF1 television crew, we flew off in a five-seater plane. Mory and I didn't have our papers. French journalists gave us their passports. Mory was "Jean-Louis" and I was "Dominique." Inside the camp, the refugees were astounded. They had never seen African personalities come to visit them, just outside doctors, perhaps. It is impossible to forget the looks of the women as they saw our well-fed, strapping frames.

In this camp, we crossed paths with representatives of Africare, the black American organization that supports and finances the continent's development. Martin Luther King's widow had wanted to come in person. Some of these activists knew me from my "Soul

Makossa" days at the Apollo in Harlem: "What are you doing here?" I explained our "Tam-Tam," our gesture for an Africa to which lawyers, athletes, and engineers could bring renewal if they wanted to. At the end of the day, we hitchhiked back. Our wandering incited an incredible climate of suspicion, even though we had come to help our compatriots. The Ethiopians didn't exactly consider themselves African. This made us think long and hard.

Throughout this whole period, traps were set for us but seldom caught us. The magazine *Jeune Afrique*, very well known on the continent, refused to take our side, wary of the political situation in Ethiopia. I insisted on it: "You could include a soft copy of 'Tam-Tam' in your next issue. Sell the whole thing for three francs extra, and what you raise can go to Ethiopia." What was I saying? "The magazine will cost more to send. We'll have to ask for special authorizations for Africa. We don't have permission to do such things." From a simple proposal that for once would show the world Africans mobilizing, a whole complicated mess arose. I was incredibly embarrassed.

But "Tam-Tam pour l'Ethiopie" resounded loudly enough to push some of my psychological obstacles out of the way. I now knew that I could get involved in ways other than losing my money or getting lost myself in the African labyrinth. Noting our success, UNICEF invited me to participate on a committee of artists and intellectuals to consider the problem of child health. Our task: to make people pay attention to the problem using new kinds of outreach materials.

Black Resonance

I N MUSIC THERE'S NO PAST and no future, just the present. I have to compose the music of my own period, not of yesterday. People have always found me "versatile" and accused me of
"pillaging." "Vampire Makossa"—I accept the judgment. How can
you create if you don't immerse yourself in the material of your
times? No creator can avoid being a vampire; painting, literature,
and the informational arts function just as music does.

In 1987, the album *Afrijazzy* became the symbol of my new
equilibrium. Coming after my long experience as a "vampire," it
took me back to myself. The "empty-bellies" from Africa to Paris
take their own paths, sometimes wary of adverse influences that
would take their hearts far from home; I pursue my path in solitude.
The continent is an inexhaustible reserve of primary musical matter.
Having married jazz and makossa, I take inspiration from sacred
music, music from the religious tradition so strong in Africa. Armstrong has not finished serving as my model, with his voice and
trumpet.

I listen with my eyes, see with my ears, speak with my voice and
my sax. Voice is an instrument that draws deeply from the wellspring
of sound, simultaneously a source of musical color and the means of
the message. Polyphonic structure is built from a complex mix of
rhythms—blues, Latin, rock, makossa, and funk—all with an African flavor. I have run in the streets of jazz in order to return to
Africa. Today I don't hesitate to scratch among the sophisticated

stores of electronic stringed instruments and electrofunk. My past versatility has made my thinking more flexible.

Electric Africa, an album of 1985 vintage, was African in a modern mode. It's today's black resonance, after the American and Caribbean. Machinery offers unimagined possibilities. This new sound is being created here in Paris, drawing on an environment different from its African roots. It's a cosmic product, invented by the Parisian Negropolitans. And they are merely the first ones. If there's anyone who knows her or his roots well, it's an African; oral tradition takes the place of books. It permits all sorts of madness, in which I move effortlessly; people have to have this kind of madness for me to get excited.

I resonate with those who surprise me: filmmakers, writers like my Cameroonian friend Blaise N'Djehoya; like Danny Laferrière, a Haitian from Montreal, for whose film *How to Make Love to a Negro Without Getting Tired* I would write the music; like Isaac de Bankolé, Maka Kotto—actors of the new generation, sharper.

But the star, the real diva, remains the music. I am a musician. Since I love it, I love sincerely as a good musician—one who plays well, who is one with his instrument. Its speed of thought fascinates me: as I improvise, the instrument is able to give birth to a cogent language. Since adolescence, I have mixed life, feelings, friendships, and my profession. Now I am trying to sort it all out, as fast as possible. I impose my own choices more brutally on the musicians who accompany me. I expect them to enrich me, to demonstrate a creative spirit. At some point, a guitarist will create a sound, an idea for a rhythmic or melodic phrase, and it's up to the band to follow along. The best improvisations need structure. Then inspiration is free to come; you always end up on your feet. Starting with a jazz standard, you can make people trip forever without ever playing the same thing. This is the heart's rhythm, life's rhythm, beating according to simple hypothesis. I love to organize sound and music on stage. I love to experience a concert at human level, closer to the public than the megaconcerts of the big megastars.

"Soul Makossa"

A band is built on the strong complicity of a gang. I've played with an incalculable number of partners. I paid them as I could; they left me for a better fee. My bands were real seedbeds of talent for Sixun, Kassav', and others.

Since 1986, I've put together a troupe at a level of quality I always dreamed about. Its creative resources astound me day after day. It is my Gang. We don't stay together just because of money; we're at ease together. I perceive their gradual assent. At the outset, perhaps, they came to me moved by self-interest, curiosity, and the desire to learn. Little by little, they took part in my vision. It was a magical process, a game of seduction, moving back and forth between love and cold calculation. Their talents drew in satellites, whom they suggested we bring into the band. The system fed on itself; thus was born the Gang, my "band of all colors."

Sissi, a singer with whom I sometimes work, introduced me to Justin. He is a pianist, and I gradually gave him responsibility for the band. A Cameroonian, he is of Bamileké ethnicity. At the Music Expo in Paris in 1986 I discovered Felix, a drummer, and Armand, a bassist. "Who are these young people who are so good-looking and who play so well?" I asked. They were two guys from eastern Cameroon, the Saballéco brothers. A little later they introduced me to Eric, a guitarist, a Frenchman of Italian origin.

The Gang pulled together. Rehearsals took place in an atmosphere of controlled fiesta—inventions, energy, professional rigor, and open merriment. This vitality became essential to me. Thanks to the party atmosphere, our creations breathed with the goodness of life. Felix and Armand are constantly creating "happenings." One day they arrived in seventeenth-century costumes, all fluorescent colors; the next day they wore panther-printed stockings. Their wit never stops. Talking about their abundant female conquests, they create words that are soon picked up from Paris to Africa—such as the expression "beaten earth" for an African woman. Their hearts wander between white women and black women according to the seasons. Felix and Armand have a rare advantage—they are a musical duo that was already functioning before I met them. This duo from the outside integrated into and enriched our beginnings as jazzmen.

Jerry, my Zairean guitarist, has stayed with me since 1971 in Zéralda. He is more than even a biological brother could be to me. When the Gang started, Felix and Armand looked askance at Jerry, who appeared to be too traditional for them. These two guys were "with it," and they had the souls of African immigrant rebels; Jerry was an old-timer who of course was incapable of playing their sound. Electrifying discussions ensued. During the course of our concerts, however, the bros discovered who Jerry the guitarist really is and what place he has in my music. They admitted it at the end of a concert in the United States: "Oh! If Jerry wanted to, he could play in America! He's invented his own language." Jerry has a sound, ideas, and a guitar technique that only he possesses; he can make his instrument into a kora, a balafon, talking drums. He's shy. He speaks little and rarely reveals himself. One day Felix and Armand hurled at him, "You can't even play the Cameroonian rhythms!" Without saying a word, Jerry took up a guitar and picked out four or five traditional Cameroonian rhythms—the ones people love best in Cameroon, a musicians' stock in trade. The guys couldn't believe it. From that day on, they have called him "Bokilo le Séquenceur."

Although my bandleader Justin started out taking the two brothers' side, he was not treated better by them. In fact, Justin got the sweet nickname "Homme de l'Ouest" ["Man of the West"] from them. Justin indeed comes from the west of Cameroon, and people from the west are considered by sidewalk radio to be the Jews of the country. They have financial power but will never be like the Doualas, the people who knew the white man first.

Peter, the trumpet player, did not escape the brothers' derision either. He's from the same country as Hugh Masekela, the South African I've always liked. Peter brings to the Gang what I hoped for: advanced technique, a knowledge of the history of jazz, and his own cultural wealth. Peter's trumpet sounds like jazz, and its color is white-black, despite apartheid. I met Peter after a phone call, during which he told me that South Africans like my music very much. The brothers there are proud that an African has succeeded in becoming well known in the United States and Europe. I like Peter's odd appearance, his maturity, the way he talks, and his clownish suspenders. I recruited Peter for *Afrijazzy* even before the Soul Makossa Gang started up.

Eric's guitar speaks its own language. A discreet man, he is generous and always tells you what he likes. Little by little, he has taken on African ways, such as not waking up on time to catch the train we planned . . .

Voice plays a primary role in our group. At my side sings N'Dedy, a Cameroonian whose timbre could wake the dead. Sometimes Florence—one of my nieces who has consummate talent—also sings with us.

All the band members have the secret to adapting to any color and traveling within any musical climate: they digest these features and then create new forms. As our proverb goes, "We're all neighborhood dogs; none of us runs faster than the others." Except the chief: the comedians in the Gang call me "Le Grand" ["Great One"], which cracks them up as soon as my back is turned. This is understandable—the Soul Makossa Gang is not a bit blasé. Its ambition is equaled only by its sense of fun. Everything is funny—a cigarette butt, Justin's fear of planes, my hypersensitivity and learned Protestant Cameroonian tone. A fundamental disagreement or some nightmare on a trip provokes an equally intense reaction.

At the same time, we work like crazy in rehearsal since our efforts shouldn't be apparent in concert. The band maneuvers like chess players, even with the audience. A concert is held like a dissertation, with an introduction, theme, and conclusion. It has its high points, like a soap opera on television. While we take our turns singing, something is happening every second. Each in turn—the band, the audience—makes its next move on the chessboard. The way we look as soon as we go on stage sets the tone. Just beforehand, we joke to create the right ambiance among us. But there is permanent tension; an unexpected guitar solo can make the current race again. Careful if it goes out!

In order to play together all these years, the band had to run like a small business. It needed a structure that could withstand the market. André Gnimagnon is a Frenchman of Beninese origin and Florence's husband, with his diploma in business. One of the managers of Africa Fête, he also became our manager. Everyone is paid per gig, but the season is spread out over the whole year. Finally I can pay everyone. Such was not always the case. How many times did I feel I'd been plucked like a hen, when I was playing under the direction of the big stars of the period! What do you have to say about that, my dear Kabasele, you who gave me so many other treasures? My African tours rarely made ends meet; the promised remuneration didn't happen, and I hadn't a dime to pay my collaborators. Decca, then Philips, and then my own labels, never made me a millionaire. Since then, I've chosen never to depend on just one recording house. I was naive and learned to be wary of monopolies, in France and Africa as well as in the United States. If you want something done right, you have to do it yourself. Bargaining with clients goes high and low; sometimes you have to give in and catch up the next time. That's usually been true in my own case; that's the price Duke paid to have his band.

Felix and Armand's look is appealing in Paris, Montreal, and Tokyo. Not so back home. Africa fears these young people, with their jeans artistically shredded. Africa remains stuck on form. Its youth lack an ideal. Modern young people in Paris affirm themselves and use their talents in music as in life. They never mention racism. They know all about Le Pen and his [xenophobic, conservative] party, which causes such a stir among the older generation, but they choose to crush such people with the weight of their youth. They are liberated in comparison to us, the old ones, stuck in our commentaries. This generation will surely bring about a new one that will affirm itself even more. It has the faith that moves mountains, creating as easily as breathing.

Felix wants to write a musical comedy for the Gang. He is already designing the costumes and refining the libretto. The troupe also expects a good vibe from me. It sometimes takes on the additional color given by dance, especially with the arrival of a young black, white, and Arab group formed recently in Elancourt, near Paris. As wanderers, we take the high roads. In our wandering, we harvest the usual travel trinkets—T-shirts, pens, glasses—from all over the world. The one who finds the best of them wins. I know this game; I played it in my youth. The closets of my apartment are full to bursting with this kind of junk, and my neighbors comment on every new toy.

The twentieth district has become my village. The newspaper vendor reserves my favorite dailies. The café owner, who inveighs against "those foreigners invading us," regularly gives me drinks for free. She still can't get over having learned from her grandchildren, who stayed in Auvergne, that I am "Manu Dibango, the great Negro, who went on TV." In this neighborhood that lacks the merest shadow of a ghetto, I breathe like a fish in water. Through the apartment housing my saxophones pass cousins from home, Parisian buddies, French-born and African, all seeking new horizons. This takes place in a kind of dynamic noncomplacency. The more you know, the more you know you know nothing. All a part of the everyday blues.

"Sonacotra Blues"

STICK TO AFRICAN MUSIC!" How many times have I heard this *diktat*, from critics as much as musicians from the continent. I have found myself stuck, labeled, locked in behind prison bars. At the beginning of the eighties, African musicians freed themselves from anonymity by the colors of their music. But this feature was then turned into a concept, on which the opinion makers began to focus. These people plant only what's in fashion according to the season; they don't let Africans escape these narrow constructs. *They* will accept *you*—or not. While they wait, they feel they need say nothing. "*Sonacotra Blues*" is the song title that fits best here. It evokes working-class immigrant residence halls in the suburbs, but it's not a sad type of blues. The prankish younger generation knows how to turn the blues around, according to their own brave fantasies.

"Stay on your continent!" is a variation on the same old theme. Popular imagination is thick-headed. Being an African musician means you play tam-tams; beyond that, no admittance. Thus the path is effectively barred to those who want to create by keeping their difference. If your head is too weak, it gives in. Having locked in the Europeans, the trap snaps shut on Africans. It's crazy the way the Afro-Parisian rumor mill finds "traitors" of all kinds. It gives Mory Kanté and Touré Kunda a beating when their stars rise into the Top 50, saying, "They've betrayed Africa." Their compatriots think badly of them. What *don't* people reproach them for in the name of their roots? Their past sticks to the soles of their shoes. Weight comes from tradition, but you need rhythm to move forward. The thing is not to get left behind by time, and we don't have any time to lose.

All this pressure has made the pot explode. Papa Wemba, Zairean king of SAPE (the Société des Ambianceurs et des Personnalités Elégantes), has altered his orchestrations. Ray Lema—another composer from Kinshasa, who now lives in Saint-Maur—has gone through the same thing. As he confided to Ariel de Bigault, actress and filmmaker: "People asked me to play a melodic line that 'sounds Pygmy.' I'd play six and they'd keep one. If it was too jazzy, they cut it out. So I'd hear two Ray Lemas. I couldn't find myself anywhere in it anymore. If there aren't a few palm trees onstage, the audience says, 'He's a fake African.' I bring neither sun nor palm trees and I get called a bad African."

Within the African community, consensus is far from reached: how to react to these pressures? It's like the fable of the Devil and God—whites perverting blacks, tradition threatened by the terrible effects of Western technology.

Gumbo Sauce

So who's the greatest traitor of them all? The French, like the members of my own race, have always tried to pin me down. A black American in France, an African in the United States, a European in Africa—it's the labeling dance. N'Djocké, the Elephant of Douala, fought to get out of his prison. Talent has no race; there simply exists a race of musicians. To be part of it, you have to have knowledge. Musicians—and composers even more so—perceive pleasant sounds around them and digest them. They like the sounds; the sounds become part of them. In Cameroon, if I buy a Mozart tape, I hear, "All right, Manu—you're helping commerce." But if I listen to it: "Oh no! Preserve us from the evil influences of the West." Listening to Mozart is betrayal. Should I deprive myself? With their voices, Pavarotti and Barbara Hendrix taught me to love opera. In my imaginary museum, they join Louis Armstrong, Duke Ellington, and Charlie Parker. I've never found better than they.

Mozart doesn't keep me from being African; the continent doesn't need this puritanical spirit. It has a rainbow of possibilities at its disposal. My much-decried versatility doesn't bother me. I'll never hesitate to start a piece with a standard introduction and continue it in other wild rhythms if that's how I feel at the moment. I like the mix. I'm a born channel-changer; I could follow shows on four TV screens simultaneously. I buy several newspapers so I can get several opinions. In music, I need to be called in many directions. I have a lot more work to do. What I wonder is whether I have it in me.

In Paris, there are Africans like me who go toward the universal. Others say they can't follow when it comes to Manu. In reality, they fear reaching universality. But without this perspective, why be born? Where are curiosity, energy, movement, if you live cloistered, your wrists and hands bound, in one spot on the earth, for seventy years? Curiosity demands means: the chance factor, plus an individual's own magnetism. With positive vibrations, you can live anywhere, or nearly—you can at least choose a more gilded cage. When Africans don't see themselves in Mory Kanté, it's their problem, not Mory's. To hear them talk, the Paris environment is "too white, too American." Yet every day they, too, drive cars and consume. We are swimming in a sea of confusion.

Simply coming from countries in which young people are satisfied to get cushy jobs and not worry about their nations' destinies doesn't make these African expatriates losers. They know who they are. They are not searching for their roots any more than the West is.

In the mists of the black suburbs of Paris, people prefer to watch over their own fires and cook their own kinds of food. Chasing after an unlikely long-stay permit, a hypothetical contract, and a glimpse of the future, they "make gumbo," as musicians back home say. In clearer terms they simply pocket fees, in a miasma of misunderstandings as thick and murky as gumbo sauce. Sticky and slick, you drink it hot. The seeds in the gumbo are fibrous, so you have to cook them a long time before you can put them into the pot with game or seafood.

These Africans all manage their own business as if they were back in their home neighborhoods. They'd do better to "make gumbo" with the French, who are so fond of it. Fortunately, this sometimes happens. The organizers of the Printemps de Bourges festival of 1985 had the smart idea of bringing together a "rainbow" band: Mino Cinelu, Charlélie Couture, Manu Dibango, Jacques Higelin, Didier Lockwood, and Tom Novembre played one another's pieces together. Now this kind of work broadens horizons. But it takes so long for everyone to find a place in all that!

Some show the way, such as Prosper Nyang of the group Xalam. Here is what he told Ariel de Bigault before his recent death: "One day in 1980, during the Dakar Jazz Festival, Kenny Clarke heard us play 'Pa'xaaf,' a Diola tune, and asked to join us. Then saxophonist Sonny Fortune and Dizzy Gillespie came along in their turn. Doudou N'Diaye Rose, the head drummer of Dakar, joined, too. We had an incredible jam. It happened on Gorée, the old slaver's island, which was even more symbolic and moving. Dizzy said, 'As a black American, I know my music comes from this land.'"

Since then, from Côte d'Ivoire to Europe, Alpha Blondy has managed to leap the hurdles and make his *Interplanetary Revolution.* He announces the arrival of a negropolitan generation braver than that of its elders. He is a man of satire. His madness suits me, makes me react more than other musicians who don't impress me—those guys are looking to you and not to me, since I already know Africa. We rarely have the chance to put our heads together. The ones you idolize are not necessarily the ones who nourish us nor those the children of Africa like so well.

I've participated in the birth of what is called "classical black African music," which has now become the point of reference. When it comes to Africa, thanks—but I've already given—since 1960, first by joining the great African musical groups and then by starting bands on the continent. Good old Fax from the Tabou in Brussels was my first piece of luck. Others followed. I've paid the price. It's the new generation's turn to give.

Among those who crowd the road to success, who will be the "elect"? Some would like to move to Paris but can't manage it. Others don't even manage to leave their own country. Those who have managed to emigrate don't always know what to do with themselves. At least their search takes place on freshly cultivated soil.

"Le 22 à Asnières"

At the beginning of the eighties, Paris offered its stage to the "empty-bellies" of the African music world, who came fresh off the boats. As the nineties dawn, the world music scene is wide open to the harbingers of Paris's black music. Japan calls to them, while the United States timidly follows the movement. The exotic label they bore so long has been left behind; their image today benefits a multicultural France. These ambassadors add their own African-style rhythms, polyphonics, and melodic wealth to the funky sauce, according to the recipes of African cuisine. Western sounds are now "under the influence," just as the American blues are. In 1960, when

Louis Armstrong triumphed in Léopoldville, Kabasele composed music in his honor. African music was and remains a music of encounters; in this lies its attractive power.

The wave of festivals that flooded the countryside in 1980 was followed by studio production with the most sophisticated of tools. The Africans of Paris were creating a new musical dimension. Going beyond London and New York, the French capital became the guiding light of black music. This soundscape was complex, its vocal color heightened by rigorous, concise rhythms. From its structured combinations rose a striking new sound. Its creators now have their feet firmly in the low-rent high-rises and rows of houses found in the Paris suburbs. With their families, weaponry, and luggage, they grow there like mushrooms. Losing nothing of their own hallucinations, they "whiten up" better than their colonized ancestors did with the help of the famous French soap Perdrix.

Paris is becoming mixed-race. Johnny Clegg says that he finds the most receptive public and the most fruitful artistic milieu here in the French capital. He's not the only one. The vibraphone goes to school with the balafon and enriches it. The tam-tam reinforces the drum-kit. Born of these sudden inventions, the musical misunderstandings between the continent and Paris finally dissipate. "Hey! Is this the 22 to Asnières?" Fernand Raynaud's brilliant routine turns into an African recipe: In order for New York to communicate with Yaoundé or Dakar, it now has to go through the Paris suburbs. The music of the sun is in fashion. In the middle of winter, street clothes look like African gowns and fabric wraps in exuberant traditional designs. Johnny Clegg plays Bercy draped in a pair of roomy pants in African tones. Distill this curious mixture in an orgy of gumbo, palm wine, and coca.

> Pata Piya picks a fruit
>
> *"When you go up into the mango tree,*
> *you take a bag with you.*
> *Because once you've picked mangoes for yourself,*
> *you also take some for the others."*

On the continent at this end of the 1980s, pirating has become a gigantic industry. Now Paris is starting to look like its practicing-ground. The African has no dough—the West is the one with the money. It makes you think.

On the horizon—"in wide screen and Dolby stereo"—the makossa beat goes off on a new track toward new tribulations. In my knapsack I'm taking my trinkets, gumbo, yams, plantains, and whiskey. In the saxophone case I have some photos for autographs, a vaccination certificate, and an old press clipping. In Paris, out of focus, his sax on his shoulder, N'Djocké, the Elephant of Douala, takes off toward new adventures . . .

So many "I's"! Above all, don't take any of this seriously. "I"—one final time—am the most surprised of all at how quickly it all went! Let's go! Nimele bolo! A nice cup of coffee awaits you. Caramba!

Honors and Distinctions

1974 Nominated for a Grammy for best album of 1973 in Hollywood and nominated for best instrumentalist.

1977 At a dedication ceremony at the Olympia, received the Trophée d'Or from Mr. Robert Galley, Minister of Cooperation, in recognition of his international career.

1985 Made an honorary citizen of Cortina d'Ampezzo, Italy.

1986 Made Knight of Arts and Letters, France. Made an honorary citizen of Torino, Italy. Received the Trophée Senghor for his extraordinary contributions in the musical domain (as author, composer, performer).

1988 Received the Knight of Order and of Valor, Cameroon.

1989 Received the Génie de la Bastille award from the Fondation ELF and the Trophée Cercle Panafricain from the Institut International de Recherche Africaine.

Discography

1960   Independence movements in Africa. Manu returned to the continent, where he visited numerous countries in both French-speaking as well as English-speaking Africa, including North Africa. His knowledge as a jazzman allowed him to appreciate the richness of traditional African culture as well as the richness of sounds.

1969–1972   He recorded several 45s.

1972   He cut his first album, *O Boso.* Then came the success of "Soul Makossa," which sold millions of copies throughout the world.

1973   His triumph at the Olympia concert hall in Paris. In the United States, "Soul Makossa" was a thunderous hit: 40,000 people saw him at Yankee Stadium, 35,000 at Madison Square Garden. He became the link among Africa, Europe, and the Americas.

1974   *Super Kumba* was recorded.

1975   *Africadélic* was recorded.

1976   *Manu 76* was recorded live at the Olympia.

1977   Manu wrote music for the films *L'Herbe Sauvage* (made in Côte d'Ivoire) and *Le Prix de la Liberté* (made in Cameroon).

1979   His trip to Jamaica proved to be a captivating encounter with reggae but also brought confrontations and reunions with jazz, soul, and salsa. A very richly colored album, *Gone Clear*, was born, featuring such prestigious musicians as Robbie Shakespeare, Geoffrey Chung, Sly Dunbar, Willie Lindo, and Ansel Collins from Jamaica; Randy and Michael Brecker, Jon Faddis, Gwen Guthrie, and Ullanda McCullouch from the United States. On this record, three black cultures melded—those of Africa, the United States, and Jamaica.

1981   The musical structure of *Gone Clear* was so effective that Manu decided to use the same musicians for his album *Ambassador*.

1982   Cameroon's most famous son returned to his country. Manu returned to Afrosound with an album entitled *Waka Juju*, containing all the musical richness of Africa. The finesse of Manu's sax playing also came through on "Douala Sérénade," the delicacy of his marimba in "Ma Marie."

1983   Manu pushed ahead without respite but was also able to bring jazz and pop standards and great classics alive. Thus, on the record *Soft and Sweet*, he recorded the songs "Poinciana," "Nature Boy," "Ni Toi Ni Moi" ["Neither You Nor I"], and "Petite Fleur" ["Little Flower"].

     Mysterious saxophone and nostalgia for the past—*Mélodies Africaines*, volumes 1 and 2, came out.

1984   First came "Abele Dance," a long 45 produced by Martin Messonnier. This title reached the top of the charts in England. Then comes the album *Surtension* [*Hypertension*], distributed by RCA, whose sound was a harbinger of future years: the "Afro-electrofunk" style.

     Manu defined himself as African and European at one and the same time. He founded the concept "négropolitain."

1985   In the Netherlands for a solidarity concert to benefit the Sahel, Manu received the shocking images of African famine like a slap in the face. On his return to Paris, he quickly brought together all the musicians he needed—present in France or not—for an adventure producing the record "Tam-Tam pour l'Ethiopie." King Sunny Adé participated by telephone from Nigeria.

     Bill Laswell, the New York producer, arrived with his whole team in Paris to produce the LP *Electric Africa*, on which, most notably, Herbie Hancock and Wally Badarou also participated. In May, along with Sting, Herbie Hancock, Seiji Ozawa, and other international personalities, Manu took part in the Parvis des Libertés et des Droits de l'Homme [Liberty and Human Rights Square], an immense humanitarian demonstration organized on the Trocadéro Plaza in Paris.

1986   *Afrijazzy* (Soul Paris, distributed by Mélodie) came out.

1988   Double live album recorded at the Francofolies as part of a
        tribute given Manu by Jean-Louis Foulquier (Buda, distrib-
        uted by Mélodie).

1989   Manu composed the music for the Franco-Canadian film
        How to Make Love to a Negro Without Getting Tired. The
        soundtrack came out on Milan (distributed by BMG). At the
        same time, Manu wrote the music for the first African car-
        toon, under the auspices of Madame Houphouët-Boigny's
        Ndaya International Foundation.

Index